כל הנשמה

Kol Haneshamah

ערב שבת

Shabbat Eve

The Reconstructionist Press
Wyncote, Pennsylvania
1993

Second Edition, 1993

Library of Congress Number: 88-63344

International Standard Book Number: 0-935457-40-1

Art by Betsy Platkin Teutsch

Book Design by Alvin Schultzberg

Composition by Bet Sha'ar Press, Inc.

Printed in the United States of America

In loving memory of
DR. LESLIE REGGEL
of Congregation Dor Hadash in Pittsburgh
whose devotion made possible the publication
of this prayerbook by the
Federation of Reconstructionist
Congregations and Havurot

With gratitude to Sylvia Dannett
a dedicated pioneer of the
Reconstructionist approach to Judaism
we dedicate the second edition

Prayerbook Commission

Rabbi Ronald Aigen
Rabbi Devora Bartnoff
Milton Bienenfeld
Lillian S. Kaplan
Marlene J. Kunin
Rabbi Joy D. Levitt
Dr. Eric Mendelsohn
Leroy C. Shuster
Rabbi David A. Teutsch, Chairperson

Ex Officio

Rabbi Arthur Green
Rabbi Mordechai Liebling
Rabbi Marcia Prager
Roger Price
Rabbi Sandy Sasso

Editorial Committee

Rabbi David A. Teutsch, *Editor-in-Chief*

Rabbi Arthur Green, *Hebrew Text*
Dr. Joel Rosenberg, *Translation*

Rabbi Deborah Brin and Rabbi Lee Friedlander, *Readings*
Kathy Green and Rabbi Brian Walt, *Home Rituals*
Betsy Platkin Teutsch, *Art*
Rabbi Sheila Peltz Weinberg, *Commentary*

Dr. Seth D. Riemer, *Editorial Assistant*

TABLE OF CONTENTS

Commentary

At the end of each section in the commentary, the authors' initials appear. Their full names are:

Ronald Aigen	Hershel Matt
Martin Buber	Eric Mendelsohn
Arthur Green	Marcia Prager
Kathy Green	Seth D. Riemer
Abraham Joshua Heschel	Rami M. Shapiro
Mordecai M. Kaplan	Steven Sager
Levi Weiman-Kelman	David A. Teutsch
Mordechai Liebling	Brian Walt

Sheila Peltz Weinberg

See also SOURCES, pages 236–245, for citations of previously published materials.

PREFACE

The task of producing a new prayerbook depends upon the work of many minds and hands. They in turn depend upon the insight and commitment of the generations of liturgists and daveners who preceded them. It would be an impossible task to mention all who have aided in this project. It would be wrong not to mention some of them.

Ludwig Nadelmann ז״ל, former president of the Jewish Reconstructionist Foundation, convened the Prayerbook Commission and appointed its first members. Charles Silberman was its first chair, and Sidney Becker, Sandy Sasso, Allan Lehmann and Ivan Caine were among its initial members. They helped to define the principles by which the reorganized Commission began its work in 1987.

Ira Eisenstein has lent his support and encouragement to the project from the outset. An editor of the 1945 prayerbook, he encouraged our efforts to produce a prayerbook for the 1990s and served as a behind-the-scenes historian who could tell us why previous decisions had been made.

The current members of the Commission have given freely of their time and energy to aid in the Commission's work. They have struggled with difficult issues and resolved them with maturity, care, and remarkable tact. When asked to take on additional work, each member has always said, "Yes." Devora Bartnoff in particular is to be thanked for her help in selecting songs, locating music and developing meditations for the book. Lillian Kaplan was an exacting proofreader.

The members of the Editorial Committee carried the brunt of the labors in producing this book. Arthur Green not only edited the inherited Hebrew text; at several critical junctures, he composed new prayers. He has also been an encyclopedic resource of Jewish liturgy. Joel Rosenberg produced a living English translation and then graciously submitted it to the vision of the Commission, revising until everyone was satisfied. He did all the translation on pages 6–148 except as otherwise indicated. Sheila Weinberg worked with a diverse group of commentators and selected with care from among their contributions. Brian Walt and Kathy Green developed the section of *zemirot* and home rituals and permitted its division into the front and back of the book. Lee Friedlander and Deborah Brin, in editing the Readings, not only carefully weighed every submission; they ranged far and wide to find the finest readings available. Betsy Platkin Teutsch joyously placed her art skills at our disposal and tailored her ideas to our needs. She has also provided support to the chairperson in countless other ways. All these editors accepted without complaint the decisions of the Prayerbook Commission and the work of their chairperson. Perhaps what is most amazing is that they each finished their work in less than ten months—a remarkable feat since all of them have busy careers and personal commitments that naturally receive their primary attention.

Many people made special contributions to this book. While correct copyright information is given by page number in the back of the book, some deserve special acknowledgment. Marcia Falk edited the brilliant Interpretive Amidah. Levi Kelman allowed extensive use of his commentary in the Friday night service. Steven Sager provided the main commentary on the structure of the service. Mel Scult culled comments from Mordecai Kaplan's published and unpublished works. Velvel Pasternak generously allowed use of his musical notation and helped with advice regarding copyrights. Sheldon Levin provided music and notation. Rivkah Walton did the first draft of the transliteration.

Seth Riemer became editorial assistant after the Commission finished its task. He has been meticulous, cheerful, unstinting, and indispensable. Mordechai Liebling has played well a critical role in managing the financial and political aspects of this project. Alvin Schultzberg of The Town House Press, together with Rabbi Miles Cohen of Bet Sha'ar Press, has patiently guided the design, typesetting, and printing.

Others who have helped include: Marcia Adelman, Penny Bar Noy, Leila Berner, Caryn Broitman, Michael M. Cohen, Jack Cohen, Susan Cohen, Dee Einhorn, Judith Kaplan Eisenstein, Bonnie Federman, Sue Frank, Evie Gechman, Nili Gold, David Golomb, Peter Herbst, Sandy Jeck, Richard Levy, Helen Nakdimen, Dora Nathanson, Yael Penkower, P'nai Or, Sharon Polsky, Zalman Schachter-Shalomi, Ben Sendrow, Rami Shapiro, Marcia Spiegel, Arnold Rachlis, Jacob Staub, Mary Wainstein, Muriel Weiss, and Elie Wise.

Those who utilize this book owe their gratitude to all those mentioned here and countless others who have worked on this book and all its predecessors. They have all been of immeasurable aid, but responsibility for the decisions concerning this prayerbook and for any errors it may contain rests solely with the Prayerbook Commission and its chair.

ברוך אתה יי אלהינו מלך העולם שהחיינו וקיימנו והגיענו לזמן הזה.

Praised are you, Yah, our God, sovereign of all worlds, who has kept us alive, and sustained us, and brought us to this time.

D.A.T.

ACKNOWLEDGMENTS

We wish to express our thanks to authors, translators, adaptors, and other copyright holders for permission to include or quote from works indicated below. Every effort has been made to identify copyright holders and obtain permission from them. Works are listed by title in alphabetical order. For additional information, see SOURCES, *pages 236–245.*

"The Amidah" by Syd Lieberman.

Amidah Tefilat Sheva, Arvit Leshabbat. A Seven-Fold Prayer of Blessings, Poems, and Meditations for the Sabbath Evening Service, by Marcia Falk. This prayer is copyright © 1989 by Marcia Falk and will appear in Marcia Falk, *The Book of Blessings: A Feminist-Jewish Reconstruction of Prayer,* forthcoming, Harper & Row, 1990. Please do not reproduce, in whole or in part, without permission. This *amidah* prayer was created by Marcia Falk, and all material in it, including blessings (in Hebrew and in English), poems, meditations, and introductory remarks, were written by Marcia Falk, with the exception of the following poems:

Mibeyt Imi (trans. from the Hebrew as "From My Mother's House") by Leah Goldberg, copyright © by Sifriat Poalim Ltd. and used by permission of Sifriat Poalim Ltd.

A Yingling Mit An Eppel in Hant (trans. from the Yiddish as "Eating an Apple") by Malka Heifetz Tussman, copyright © 1958 by Malka Heifetz Tussman and used by permission of Joseph Tussman.

Ikh Bin Froy (trans. from the Yiddish as "I am Woman") by Malka Heifetz Tussman, copyright © 1949 by Malka Heifetz Tussman and used by permission of Joseph Tussman.

Beḥol davar yesh lefaḥot sheminit . . . (trans. from the Hebrew as "In everything, there is at least an eighth . . .") by Leah Goldberg, copyright © 1971 by Sifriat Poalim Ltd. and used by permission of Sifriat Poalim Ltd.

Hakarmel Ha'inireh (trans. from the Hebrew as "The Invisible Carmel") by Zelda, copyright © 1971 by Hakibbutz Hameuchad Ltd.

Bletter (trans. from the Yiddish as "Leaves") by Malka Heifetz Tussman, copyright © 1972 by Malka Heifetz Tussman and used by permission of Joseph Tussman.

"Each of Us Has a Name" is a translation by Marcia Falk of a Hebrew poem by Zelda. *Leḥol Ish Yesh Shem* is from *Shirey Zelda,* © 1985 by Hakibbutz Hameuchad Ltd.

Hadliku Ner (trans. from the Hebrew as "Light a Candle") by Zelda, copyright © 1967 by Hakibbutz Hameuchad Ltd.

Hageshem harishon . . . (trans. from the Hebrew as "The first rain . . .") by Zelda, copyright © 1981 by Hakibbutz Hameuchad Ltd.

All translations of the above are by Marcia Falk.

"Angels" by Rabbi Rami M. Shapiro.

"An Appendix to the Vision of Peace" from *Greater Tranquility* by Yehuda Amichai, translated by Glenda Abramson and Tudor Parfitt. Copyright © 1983 by Yehuda Amichai. Reprinted by permission of Harper & Row, Publishers, Inc.

Arvit Leshabbat. Translation, Introduction, & Commentary by Rabbi Levi Weiman-Kelman, copyright © 1986.

"Blessed is the match" translated from the poem by Hannah Szenes.

"Dirge Without Music" by Edna St. Vincent Millay. From *Collected Poems,* Harper & Row. Copyright © 1928, 1955 by Edna St. Vincent Millay and Norma Millay Ellis. Reprinted by permission.

"*Dodi Li*"—lyrics: traditional; music: Nira Chen; copyright © by the composer, Israel.

"*Esa Eynay*"—lyrics: traditional; music by Rabbi Shlomo Carlebach. Used by permission of the composer.

Exodus and Revolution by Michael Walzer, copyright © 1985 by Basic Books, Inc., Publishers.

"The Five Stages of Grief" is reprinted from *The Five Stages of Grief,* Poems by Linda Pastan, by permission of W. W. Norton & Company, Inc. Copyright © 1978 by Linda Pastan.

"I Know Not Your Ways" translated by Marcia Falk from a poem by Malka Heifetz Tussman, copyright © 1977 by Marcia Falk. Used by permission.

"I look up to the sky and the stars. . . ." This translation of a poem by Shmuel Hanagid appeared previously in *Society Hill Synagogue Prayer Supplement,* edited by Ivan Caine.

"I Shall Sing to the Lord a New Song," Ruth H. Sohn, copyright © 1981.

"In Praise / GENESIS 1, 2" by Ruth F. Brin in *Harvest: Collected Poems and Prayers,* The Reconstructionist Press, copyright © 1986 by Ruth Firestone Brin.

"The Intention" by Margaret Torrie. Taken from *All In the End is Harvest* edited by Agnes Whitaker, published and copyright © 1984 by Darton, Longman and Todd Ltd. / CRUSE and is used by permission of the publishers.

"It Is Up To Us" by Rabbi Rami M. Shapiro.

"*Kol Ha'olam Kulo.*" Words by Naḥman of Bratslav. Music by Baruch Chait.

"*Lo Yisa Goy*" music by Shalom Altman. Used by permission of Jeremy Altman.

"Merger" by Judy Chicago from *The Dinner Party.* Copyright © 1979 by Judy Chicago. Reprinted by permission of Doubleday, a division of Bantam, Doubleday, Dell Publishing Group, Inc.

"The Peace of Wild Things," by Wendell Berry, from *Collected Poems,* copyright © 1985 by Wendell Berry. Published by North Point Press and reprinted by permission.

"Receive and Transmit II" by Rabbi Rami M. Shapiro.

"A Sense of Your Presence" by Ruth F. Brin, in *Harvest: Collected Poems and Prayers,* The Reconstructionist Press, copyright © 1986 by Ruth Firestone Brin.

"*Shabbat Hamalkah*" in *Likrat Shabbat,* copyright © 1977 by The Prayer Book Press of Media Judaica, Inc.

"*Shalom Aleyḥem.*" Traditional lyrics, translated and adapted by Rabbi Burt Jacobson. Music by Israel Goldfarb.

"Some Blessings," copyright © 1988, Marge Piercy, Middlemarsh, Inc.

"Song of the Sabbath" by Kadia Molodowsky, translated by Jean Valentine. From *A Treasury of Yiddish Poetry* edited by Irving Howe and Eliezer Greenberg. Copyright © 1969 by Irving Howe and Eliezer Greenberg. Reprinted by permission of Henry Holt and Company, Inc.

"Strange is our situation here upon earth." From the writings of Albert Einstein.

"*Te Deum*" copyright © 1977 by Marie Syrkin Reznikoff. Reprinted from *Poems 1937–1975* with the permission of Black Sparrow Press.

Passages collected and edited by Martin Buber are from *Ten Rungs: Hasidic Sayings,* translated by Olga Mark, Schocken Books, copyright © 1977.

"To light candles" translated from the poem by Zelda.

"To My Father." Believed to be the work of Blaga Dmitrova.

"Trees" by Howard Nemerov, from *The Collected Poems of Howard Nemerov.* The University of Chicago Press, copyright © 1977. Reprinted by permission of the author.

"Unending Love" by Rabbi Rami M. Shapiro.

"*Veha'er Eyneynu*" music by Rabbi Shlomo Carlebach. Used by permission of the composer.

"We All Stood Together," by Merle L. Feld, copyright © 1985. Merle Feld is a playwright whose works include *The Gates are Closing* and *Moving Into the Light.*

"We Mothers" from *The Seeker* by Nelly Sachs. Copyright © 1970 by Farrar, Straus and Giroux, Inc. Reprinted by permission of Farrar, Straus and Giroux, Inc.

"Wellfleet Sabbath." From *Available Light* by Marge Piercy. Copyright © 1988 by Middlemarsh, Inc. Reprinted by permission of Alfred A. Knopf, Inc.

"Who is Like You" by Rabbi Rami M. Shapiro.

"Wildpeace" by Yehuda Amichai, translated by Chana Bloch and Ariel Bloch.

"*Yevareḥeḥa*"—lyrics: traditional; music: David Weinkrantz, copyright © by Osnat Publ. Ltd. Israel.

Sylvia Heschel gave permission for use of works by Abraham Joshua Heschel.

INTRODUCTION

This experimental edition launches a new series of Reconstructionist prayerbooks. In the democratic spirit of this movement, we ask you to use it for several months and then to let us know what works and what doesn't, what you find inspiring and what you find problematical. Your responses will shape the *Siddur for Shabbat and Festivals* that will follow.

When the Jewish Reconstructionist Foundation published the *Sabbath Prayer Book* in 1945, it was a revolutionary event. In fact, a picture of some rabbis who burned it as heresy landed on the front page of the *New York Times.* That book plays a critical part in the legacy of the first generation of Reconstructionists. It rests on four principles: reverence for the traditional siddur (prayerbook); use of the vast literature of Judaism; cognizance of contemporary problems and aspirations; and courage to produce new liturgy and edit the traditional liturgy in order to be true to contemporary Jewish sensibilities and moral vision.

The series of prayerbooks launched in 1945 deleted references to Jewish chosenness, to *Mashiaḥ ben David* (Messiah son of David), to hope for the reinstitution of sacrifices, to individual reward and punishment, and to bodily resurrection. It assumed that not every word of Scripture is factual and divinely ordained. Those prayerbooks, edited by Mordecai Kaplan, Eugene Kohn, Ira Eisenstein, and Milton Steinberg, have provided an invaluable legacy to this generation of worshippers. The new prayerbook remains faithful to their principles. In fact, they helped to inspire the current generation's efforts by asserting that each generation should act in light of its own Jewish sensibilities, moral strivings, and spiritual search.

By 1980 a consensus on the need for a new Reconstructionist prayerbook had emerged. The situation of North American

Jewry has changed remarkably since the 1940s. Then Jews were struggling to assimilate into North American society. Today many North Americans are trying to find their way into Judaism. In the 1940s the horror of the Holocaust and the emergence of the State of Israel had not yet redefined the Jewish sense of self, and the ethnic awakening of Jews had not yet begun. The language of prayer had not yet been affected by the growing informality of American manners. There was no way of anticipating the smaller groups that would join in prayer, the return to lay leadership in worship, the growing desire for a sense of inclusion. Many of the traditional metaphors found in prayer were considered necessary conventions by those who had grown up with them. Today many Jews see those metaphors as more outdated and foreign than ever before. English usage, too, has changed considerably in the last forty years. Thus there was substantial agreement about the need to change.

The exact nature of the changes needed remained elusive, however. After just a few meetings and discussions in 1981 and 1982, the prayerbook project was suspended until 1987, when the Prayerbook Commission was reorganized and editorial work began. The composition of the Prayerbook Commission itself is noteworthy. For the first time in Jewish history, the body overseeing the development of a Jewish prayerbook contains a roughly equal number of rabbis and laypeople, as well as equal involvement of men and women. The Reconstructionist Rabbinical Association and Federation of Reconstructionist Congregations and Havurot appointed commission members with the intention of representing the diverse views and practices of those who will use the new book. The lively discussions of the commission often grew out of efforts to understand the differing sensibilities of its members and to make room for them within the prayerbook while maintaining its coherence as a unified liturgy.

The five-year hiatus that began in 1982 provided an opportunity for a consensus around several issues to emerge. Norms and conventions regarding gender-neutral language have stabilized. Acceptance of diverse styles of worship and ritual within our movement has moved steadily forward. The desire for both a full Hebrew text and contemporary poetic additional readings has grown. Furthermore, it has become steadily more evident that the most rapidly growing constituency for the new prayerbook is comprised of Jews who are finding their way to fuller Jewish lives despite scanty Jewish educations and scarce memories of powerful experiences of worship and ritual. They are discovering for themselves the treasures of learning and action, spiritual discipline and ritual in Judaism. Fears that more traditional worship styles inevitably carry with them more traditional theology have been put to rest.

The members of the editorial committee worked individually on the areas assigned them, with the product of their efforts coming back to the Prayerbook Commission for comment. The editorial committee has not only brought an extraordinary array of knowledge, skills, and insights to bear on the project; it has brought varied spiritual lives and personal tastes as well. Furthermore, its members have been tolerant of the Prayerbook Commission's need to retain editorial control. We have aimed to produce a book with a central core that unifies through style and basic theological assumptions while allowing the multi-vocal nature of the collective enterprise of Jewish prayer to emerge. What that has meant in more specific terms can be illustrated by looking at the individual parts of the prayerbook:

HEBREW. The new Hebrew text was shaped by several influences: The Sephardic and Ashkenazic texts of *Kabbalat Shabbat,* the theological considerations that frame Reconstructionism, and the recent additions to the service from around the world. Hebrew texts that were omitted for non-theological reasons in the first Reconstructionist prayerbook have been restored. Sections of the Song of Songs, traditionally recited on Friday evening, have been added to *Kabbalat Shabbat,* providing rich and vivid imagery. Several newly composed texts, including an additional version of the *Aleynu,* have been added. They respond to several needs: to include suitable references to the Holocaust and the founding of the State of Israel, to further explicate the movement's commitment to pluralism and universalism, and to respond to lessons learned from feminism. Some of these changes are subtle, and some add options. The result is a Hebrew text suitable for use either by itself or in conjunction with English translation and readings.

TRANSLITERATION. Since a prayerbook is of little use if it is not accessible, and since many who could grow into its use have virtually no Hebrew language skills, transliteration has been placed adjacent to the Hebrew. All the parts of the service that are frequently sung are transliterated. This is done as a bridge for newcomers, encouraging their participation in worship. It is hoped that such participation will inspire people to learn Hebrew for themselves: Full participation in Jewish culture requires Hebrew literacy.

COMMENTARY. A large number of those who will use the new prayerbook have little knowledge of the structure or history of the siddur. In many cases they have had little opportunity to experience prayer as deeply moving and life-shaping. The commentary addresses that reality in several ways. It points out the underlying structure of the liturgy. It notes places where the new prayerbook differs from the traditional siddur and explains why. It provides contemporary interpretations and applications of the traditional liturgy and explores the meaning of particular terms and literary forms. The commentary will help to open the prayerbook to people who might otherwise find communal worship alienating, or who find private prayer incomprehensible. It can help all of us to continue learning about the liturgy.

The explanations at the bottom of the page are divided into five categories: Comments beginning with *Hebrew words* explain the meaning of those words. *Notes* are short explanations. *Commentary* discusses liturgical structure, literary forms, and the meaning of particular prayers. *Kavanot* are intended to shape the spiritual intention, the inner direction with which prayers are spoken. *Derash* is a homiletical form that makes a moral point or provides a popular interpretation.

TRANSLATION. Influenced by the power of the King James translation of the Bible and by a desire for grandeur and majesty in worship, prayerbook translations in English have had an archaic flavor about them until quite recently. Moving toward a contemporary, vivid, yet elegant translation required the hand of a poet steeped in Jewish tradition and American idiom. Joel Rosenberg's efforts were complicated by the decision to make the translation completely gender-neutral. A solution to this and similar problems grew out of complex interpretations weaving together the poetic, the theological, and the midrashic. These sources provided the foundation from which the new translation emerged.

יהוה. The most difficult translation issue is the question of God-language. The classical translation of the YHVH name of God is Lord, which is a masculine noun that does not work in terms of gender. It does not work as living imagery. Furthermore, it is not consistent with a theology that stresses God's immanence—God made manifest through human action, through nature, and through the workings of the human heart. After discussing many alternatives, the Commission agreed to follow a custom common in Sephardic prayerbooks. Everywhere that the Tetragrammaton or *Adonay* appears, they place an additional appellation above or below it. The rabbis often based these appellations on the thirteen divine attributes, but did not limit themselves to the attributes. That is the format we have used in the English translation. Wherever "*Adonay*/Lord" would have been said, we have written Yah above the line and another name for God below it.

Several reasons underlie this decision: It solves the problem many people have in relating to "Lord." It conveys the specialness, mystery, and ineffability of the divine. It utilizes an ancient name of God drawn from the first half of the Tetragrammaton. It is a name that we all know from saying, "hallelu-Yah!"—literally, "Praise Yah!" It allows us to explore the many different aspects of divinity infused in the world. It clearly demarcates where the Hebrew uses the Tetragrammaton. It provides for local autonomy, allowing each congregation to use what is above the line, what is below the line, or an altogether different alternative.

READINGS. The readings in the prayerbook are selected with attention to significant literary quality, to a combination of clarity and complexity, to their ability to evoke images and feelings, and to their ability to wear well with repeated use. The readings are not didactic; they are meant to help us discover what is ready to be revealed within ourselves.

Furthermore, the readings play an important role by providing a counterbalance to the more traditional Hebrew. Changing huge sections of the Hebrew liturgy would sever our roots in traditional prayer. So missing themes must find their place elsewhere, and the additional readings are a natural place for them. For example, the voices of women emerge in the readings; women's voices were absent in the traditional liturgy. That has meant not strained jargon nor a separatist viewpoint, but rather the expression of hopes and perceptions that all of us can grow into sharing. This is a transitional time in the movement toward inclusive language and imagery. Such language and imagery can only emerge over time in a prayer community. We affirm that journey through time and recognize that it will carry both the English and the Hebrew of the siddur far beyond what we in our lifetimes will witness. Still, we hope that some of what we have done will become a lasting part of Jewish tradition.

No prayerbook's readings can be expected to be comprehensive. They will neither reflect the continuously changing panorama of world events, nor reflect every mood, insight, or theological nuance. Furthermore, many of the readings suitable for use by congregation or havurah do not hold up well with frequent repetition. This makes them no less suitable for occasional use; they should be used in a disposable format rather than add their weight to the pages of a prayerbook. We hope that leaders will choose to use the readings here often and still recognize that a continuous search for supplemental sources will enrich the liturgical experience.

SONGS. For many, singing provides a sense of belonging and active participation in public worship. One purpose of this section of the prayerbook is to provide a wide choice of songs that can be a part of Kabbalat Shabbat. The decision to include musical notation results partly from the Reconstructionist commitment to music as a part of Jewish culture, a commitment fostered by Judith Kaplan Eisenstein. It also partly results from the effort to increase the accessibility of songs of the tradition.

DESIGN. The design of this prayerbook highlights the meaning of the text and suggests fresh ways of thinking about it. Design should enhance the text rather than compete with it. Most of the artwork in this siddur is calligraphic because representational art would be too literal for use in a siddur and because such art has not been a frequently used Jewish form. While including artwork in a siddur is uncommon, it reflects a deep commitment to all aspects of Jewish civilization. That commitment has been the hallmark of the Reconstructionist movement.

The overall appearance of a prayerbook contributes to the aesthetic experience. We have done our best to produce clean, spare pages. They are meant to be both highly readable and pleasing to the eye. In general, we have placed the Hebrew on the left side of the page rather than on the customary right. This is done partly for aesthetic reasons and partly to allow the beginnings of lines to be near each other for those moving back and forth between Hebrew and English. We feel confident that once people move beyond their initial surprise, they will quickly feel comfortable with the layout.

A USER'S GUIDE. The design of this siddur makes it easy to use. Relatively inexperienced service leaders and daveners should find that the rubrics guide them smoothly through such questions as: Where do I stand or sit? Where can I put extra readings? Which themes belong where? We hope that the siddur's rubrics will provide a sufficient guide to use, but we recognize that local *minhagim* (customs) vary so widely that all of them could not possibly be mentioned. We hope that differing local customs will continue to flourish.

A COLLECTIVE OF DISTINCTIVE INDIVIDUALS. By now it should be clear that each group of editors who worked on a section of the prayerbook had a different charge. I believe that this process has produced a book in which many voices can be heard. No effort has been made to mute the distinctiveness of those voices. The members of the choir, however, were selected with an eye to the range and timbre of their voices. The distinctiveness of the soloists at any moment is therefore compatible with the liturgical choir. It will be up to each *sheliaḥ tzibur* (service leader) to decide which voices should be heard on any given day. The wide range of choices should allow each congregation to use the new prayerbook in a way continuous with previous congregational practice. It is hoped that the book will also stimulate congregations and minyanim to try new things, to stretch themselves a bit. The prayerbook was never a homogenized entity. It always included the voices of theists and panentheists, mystics and scholars, pietists and traditionalists. That multi-vocality is just as present in our book. We hope that your voice, too, will be heard in the prayers that fly off the new siddur's pages.

WHERE DO WE GO FROM HERE? This first section of the new prayerbook was produced by an extraordinarily talented group of editors and overseen by a thoughtful and hardworking Prayerbook Commission. It is, however, an experimental edition. Our movement, based upon democratic principles, could never consider a prayerbook our own unless Reconstructionists could comfortably and effectively use it. There are significant changes in the new siddur, and we recognize that it will take time to become comfortable with it.

After that initial break-in period, the Commission looks forward to feedback from the users of the experimental edition. Your comments will be useful after you have been using it regularly in worship for a few months. Responses will be used to reshape the service for Shabbat eve and the rest of the siddur project. A partnership of scholars and lay leaders, rabbis and shul-goers marks our movement. That partnership has been the impetus for this book, and it will shape the book's development and deepen with its use. We look forward to your guidance.

KOL HANESHAMAH. The name of the new siddur comes from Psalm 150—*Kol haneshamah tehalel Yah.* That is often translated, "Let every soul praise God." But *kol haneshamah* could also mean, "all the soul." Let all of the soul offer praise. By changing one letter (kaf to kuf), it would sound the same but become "the voice of the soul." Let it be the soul's voice that offers praise. These are our hopes for this book. Let everyone who opens it find here the means to praise God. Let those who use it regularly fill their souls with the divine. And let us together give voice to the divine in ways that transform us and our world.

DAVID A. TEUTSCH
Chair, Prayerbook Commission

Introduction to the Second Edition

This Second Edition is the result of demand for *Kol Haneshemah: Erev Shabbat*, which has exceeded our highest expectations. The original intention of the editors was to let *Kol Haneshemah: Erev Shabbat* go out of print when the *Shabbat Veḥagim* siddur became available; however, we have been overwhelmed by requests for additional copies.

This is the first edition in a long-lasting hardcover binding, signaling the decision that this volume will remain available. Various minor errors in the original edition have been corrected. In all other respects the second edition is identical to the first.

NOTES ON USAGE

Hebrew Pronunciation. The pronunciation in this siddur follows current Israeli usage. Accordingly, Hebrew words are accented on the final syllable unless otherwise noted. Where the stress is not on the last syllable of a word, the stressed syllable is marked with a caret (×֫). In biblical passages where there are cantillation marks, those marks replace the caret in marking the stressed syllable. The *kamatz katan* (pronounced "o" as in "store") is marked with this sign: ×ׇ.

Transliteration. Where Hebrew words are not accented on the final syllable, this is indicated by underlining the accented syllable in the transliteration. Use of periods and capital letters roughly follows Hebrew sentence structure. Generally, no other punctuation will occur. Below is a table of Hebrew letters and vowels with their English equivalents.

Consonants

א	(not pronounced)	ל	l
בּ	b	ם מ	m
ב	v	ן נ	n
ג	g (as in "go")	ס	s
ד	d	ע	(not pronounced)
ה	h	פּ	p
ו	v	ף פ	f
ז	z (as in "Zion")	ץ צ	tz (as in "mitzvah")
ח	ḥ (as in "*ḥazan*")	ק	k
ט	t	ר	r
י	y	שׁ	sh
ךּ כּ	k	שׂ	s
ך כ	ḥ (as in "*baruḥ*")	ת תּ	t

June 16 8:00

Kiedusa 28

Nor villa

09/11/38

Vowels

אֵ / אֶ / אֱ / אְ	e (as in "bed")
אַ / אֲ / אָ	a (as in "are")
אוֹ / אֹ / אָ / אֳ	o (as in "store")
אוּ / אֻ	u (as in "put")
אִי / אִ	i (as in "sit")

Diphthongs and Glides

אֵי	ey (as in "they")
אֵא / אֵה	ey (as in "they"; only at the end of a word)
אַי	ay (as in "bayou")
וּי	uwi (u + i, pronounced rapidly together)
וֹי	oy (as in "toy")

Hebrew words whose transliterations have become standard or familiar English have been retained. Examples: Shabbat, siddur, sukkah, Kiddush. In these cases the doubling of the middle consonant has been kept even though the system of transliteration used here does not require it.

קבלת שבת

The *Kabbalat Shabbat* service was created by the Kabbalists (Jewish mystics) of Safed in the sixteenth century and was almost universally accepted by Jewish communities. Though a relatively recent innovation in Jewish liturgy, it probably springs from ancient customs such as those of R. Ḥanina and R. Yanay (third century Palestine). The Talmud records that at sunset on Shabbat eve, R. Ḥanina would stand dressed in fine garments and say, "Come, let us go forth to welcome the Sabbath queen." R. Yanay, in festive attire, would exclaim, "Come, Oh bride! Come, Oh bride!"

The augmented version of *Kabbalat Shabbat* presented here is intended to offer variety within a traditional form of worship. The prayer-leader (*sheliaḥ tzibur*) should construct a service by selecting elements from among the introductory hymns, passages from the Song of Songs, Psalms, and additional readings to be found below. For additional readings see pages 186–196, 205–206, 211. A.G./S.S.

צדקה / *tzedakah.* As God created for six days, so too do we labor. Just before Shabbat—the time of divine and human rest—begins, some of us engage in *tzedakah* to complete the work of renewing creation. The root letters of the word *tzedakah* translate as "justice" or "righteousness." By giving to those in need, we help to right a wrong and thus share responsibility for creation. In some homes the *pushka* or *tzedakah* box stands next to the Shabbat candles to receive the last coins of our workaday lives.

Some families may direct their *tzedakah* to a particular charity, organization, or cause. Family discussion and reconsideration of choices from time to time may heighten the meaning of the act. Some households create their own *pushka* and adorn it with biblical verses and illustration.

Rabbi Elazar would always give a coin to a poor person before praying. In explanation he would quote, "I shall behold your face *betzedek,* in righteousness" (Psalm 17:15). B.W./K.G.

HADLAKAT NEROT SHABBAT / LIGHTING SHABBAT CANDLES

Candles are traditionally lit in the home. Many communities also light candles together at the beginning of the Kabbalat Shabbat *service.* *For additional readings see pages 186–187.*

To light candles in all the worlds—
that is Shabbat.
To light Shabbat candles
is a soul-leap pregnant with potential
into a splendid sea, in it the mystery
of the fire of sunset.
Lighting the candles transforms
my room into a river of light,
my heart sets in an emerald waterfall.

Zelda (anonymous translator)

* *

As the great doors of night are opening
we come into the clean quiet room of Shabbat.
Let us be thankful, as we light these candles
like eyes of holiness, for this moment of peace.

Let us savor the fruit of the vine,
the blood of the earth that quickens us.

Let us be thankful for grain, fruit of grasses
that feed the cow, the gazelle and us.

Let us be grateful for the children and the work
of the week that are our own fruitfulness.

Let us as we eat never forget that food comes
from the earth we must cherish and heal
through labor we must respect and reward.

Marge Piercy

הדלקת נרות שבת

Candles are traditionally lit in the home. Many communities also light candles together at the beginning of the Kabbalat Shabbat *service.*

לְהַדְלִיק נֵרוֹת בְּכָל־הָעוֹלָמוֹת —
זוֹהִי שַׁבָּת.
לְהַדְלִיק נֵרוֹת־שַׁבָּת
זוֹהִי קְפִיצַת־נֶפֶשׁ הֲרַת נְצוּרוֹת
לְיָם נֶהְדָּר, שֶׁיֵּשׁ בָּהּ מִסְתּוֹרִין
שֶׁל אֵשׁ־הַשְּׁקִיעָה.
בְּהַדְלִיקִי הַנֵּרוֹת יֵהָפֵךְ
חֶדְרִי לִנְהַר דִּי־נוּר,
בְּאַשְׁדּוֹת בָּרֶקֶת שׁוֹקֵעַ לִבִּי.

NOTE. While minimally we light two new Shabbat candles, we may choose to light more. Some families light a candle for each member.

The physical motions associated with candle-lighting are unique to each of us and take on individual meaning. Some lift their hands over the flames and toward themselves as though drawing the light of Shabbat into themselves. Others lift their hands over the flames six times as though to incorporate each day of the week into Shabbat.

Many people cover their eyes while saying the blessing. In this way they maintain the customary order of blessing before acting—they delay their enjoyment of the lights. Covering the eyes also symbolizes our need to avert our eyes from the blinding light of the divine.

Many of us set aside the contemplative moments before and after candle-lighting as a time for our own private prayers and intentions.

B.W./K.G./D.A.T.

Blessed are you, YAH / SOURCE OF LIGHT our God, sovereign of all worlds, who has made us holy with your mitzvot, and commanded us to kindle the Shabbat light.

* *

Blessed is the match that's consumed in kindling a flame.
Blessed is the flame that burns in the secret depths of the heart.

Hannah Szenes (anonymous translator)

* *

Almighty God,
Grant me and all my loved ones
A chance truly to rest on this Shabbat.
May the light of the candles drive out from among us
The spirit of anger, the spirit of harm.
Send your blessings to my children,
That they may walk in the ways of your Torah, your light.

Shas Tkhines (anonymous translator)

YEDID NEFESH / SOUL BELOVED

This translation can be sung to the same melody as the Hebrew.

You who love my soul,
Sweet source of tenderness
Take my inner nature
And shape it to your will.
Like a darting deer
I will flee to you.
Before your glorious presence
Humbly do I bow.
Let your sweet love
Delight me with its thrill.
Because no other dainty
Will my hunger still. ↩

The candles are now lit. After candle-lighting, the following blessing is recited:

בָּרוּךְ אַתָּה יהוה אֱלֹהֵינוּ מֶלֶךְ הָעוֹלָם אֲשֶׁר קִדְּשָׁנוּ
בְּמִצְוֹתָיו וְצִוָּנוּ לְהַדְלִיק נֵר שֶׁל שַׁבָּת׃

Baruḥ atah adonay eloheynu meleḥ ha'olam asher kideshanu bemitzvotav vetzivanu lehadlik ner shel shabbat.

YEDID NEFESH

Transliteration can be found on page 11.

How splendid is your light
Which worlds do reflect!
My soul is worn from craving
For your love's delight.
Please, good God, do heal her
And show to her your face,
So my soul can see you
And bathe in your grace.
There she will find strength
And healing in this sight.
Her joy will be complete then,
Eternal her delight.

What pity stirs in you
Since days of old, my God!
Be kind to me your own child
Begotten by your love.
For long and longing hours
I yearned for your embrace, ↩

COMMENTARY. *Yedid Nefesh* was written by Rabbi Eleazar Azikri of Safed. A love song of the soul to God, it achieved great popularity in Sephardic communities, where it was included in the daily prayerbook. Hasidic custom adopted it for use as an introduction to Shabbat. The poet speaks to God in most intimate terms as lover and parent, but also as shining light of the universe. The longing for God is fulfilled for "the time has come" as God spreads over the world the great *sukkat shalom,* canopy of peace, which is Shabbat.

The traditional Hebrew text of *Yedid Nefesh* presented here differs in several places from Azikri's original. Most notably, this version substitutes in the second verse "Eternal her delight" for "She shall be your handmaiden forever." Here tradition seems to have improved on the author's work! A.G.

יְדִיד נֶפֶשׁ אָב הָרַחֲמָן מְשׁוֹךְ עַבְדְּךָ אֶל רְצוֹנֶךָ:
יָרוּץ עַבְדְּךָ כְּמוֹ אַיָּל יִשְׁתַּחֲוֶה אֶל מוּל הֲדָרֶךָ:
תֶּעֱרַב לוֹ יְדִידוּתֶךָ מִנֹּפֶת צוּף וְכָל־טָעַם:

הָדוּר נָאֶה זִיו הָעוֹלָם נַפְשִׁי חוֹלַת אַהֲבָתֶךָ:
אָנָּא אֵל נָא רְפָא נָא לָהּ בְּהַרְאוֹת לָהּ נֹעַם זִיוֶךָ:
אָז תִּתְחַזֵּק וְתִתְרַפֵּא וְהָיְתָה לָהּ שִׂמְחַת עוֹלָם:

וָתִיק יֶהֱמוּ נָא רַחֲמֶיךָ וְחוּסָה נָּא עַל בֵּן אֲהוּבֶךָ:
כִּי זֶה כַּמָּה נִכְסֹף נִכְסַפְתִּי לִרְאוֹת בְּתִפְאֶרֶת עֻזֶּךָ:
אֵלֶּה חָמְדָה לִבִּי חוּסָה נָּא וְאַל תִּתְעַלָּם:

הִגָּלֶה נָא וּפְרוֹשׂ חֲבִיבִי עָלַי אֶת־סֻכַּת שְׁלוֹמֶךָ:
תָּאִיר אֶרֶץ מִכְּבוֹדֶךָ נָגִילָה וְנִשְׂמְחָה בָּךְ:
מַהֵר אָהוּב כִּי בָא מוֹעֵד וְחָנֵּנוּ כִּימֵי עוֹלָם:

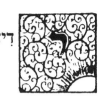

To see my light in your light
Basking in your grace.
My heart's desire is
To harmonize with yours
Do not conceal your pity
Hide not that light of yours.

Help, my lover, spread
Your canopy of peace,
Enfold all human beings.
Give all pain surcease.
Your presence on this earth plane
Do make known to us
And we shall respond then
With song and with dance.
Rush, my love, be quick,
The time for love has come,
Let your gentle favor
Grace us as of old.

Eleazar Azikri (translated by Zalman Schachter-Shalomi)

COMMENTARY. The first letter of each verse spells out יהוה, the four-letter name of God. That name subsumes and unites all the descriptions which Jewish tradition has evolved in its quest for the divine. Jews may once have commonly pronounced יהוה, but they have avoided doing so since at least the third century B.C.E. The traditional vocalization "Yahweh" can be understood as, "He causes to exist," or just, "He is!" It also resembles God's enigmatic words to Moses at the burning bush: "*Ehyeh Asher Ehyeh*—I Am Who I am" (Exodus 3:14). Thus יהוה hints at the absurdity of assigning a name to an ineffable divinity. M.P.

Yedid nefesh av haraḥaman meshoḥ avdeḥa el retzoneḥa.
Yarutz avdeḥa kemo ayal yishtaḥaveh el mul hadareḥa.
Te'erav lo yediduteḥa minofet tzuf veḥol ta'am.

Hadur na'eh ziv ha'olam nafshi ḥolat ahavateḥa.
Ana el na refa na lah beharot lah no'am ziveḥa.
Az titḥazek vetitrapey vehayetah lah simḥat olam.

Vatik yehemu na raḥameḥa veḥusah na al ben ahuveḥa.
Ki zeh kamah niḥsof niḥsafti lirot betiferet uzeḥa.
Eleh ḥamdah libi ḥusah na ve'al titalam.

Higaley na ufros ḥavivi alay et sukkat shelomeḥa.
Ta'ir eretz mikvodeḥa nagilah venismeḥah baḥ.
Maher ahuv ki va mo'ed veḥonenu kimey olam.

אל נא רפא נא לה. A quotation from Moses's prayer to heal Miriam, "God, please heal her" (Numbers 12:13). God is sought as the source of spiritual healing—soul healing. In union with the divine we find release from the pain of the futile cycle of searching and disappointment. Shabbat is our refuge of acceptance, our shelter from cravings and strivings. S.P.W.

DERASH. Our yearning for salvation is the human form of the will to live, which is cosmic and characteristic of all living beings. In our case the will to live is the will to abundant and harmonious living. . . . Human nature is part of the larger world of nature, and our salvation can only be conceived as a manifestation of a divine power both within and beyond us.
M.M.K. (ADAPTED)

SHABBAT HAMALKAH / THE SHABBAT QUEEN

This translation can be sung to the same melody as the Hebrew.

The sun on the treetops no longer is seen;
Come, gather to welcome the Sabbath, our queen!

Behold her descending, the holy, the blessed,
And with her the angels, of peace and of rest.

Draw near, O queen, and here abide;
Draw near, draw near, O Sabbath bride.

Peace be unto you, O angels of peace.

Ḥayim Naḥman Bialik (adapted from a translation by A. Irma Cohon)

NOTE. *Shabbat Hamalkah* is the work of Ḥayim Naḥman Bialik, the great poet of the Hebrew national revival. His poem, like *Yedid Nefesh,* was not originally written for the synagogue, but it has achieved great popularity as a song of welcome to Shabbat. A.G.

שַׁבָּת הַמַּלְכָּה

הַחַמָּה מֵרֹאשׁ הָאִילָנוֹת נִסְתַּלְּקָה.
בֹּ֫אוּ וְנֵצֵא לִקְרַאת שַׁבָּת הַמַּלְכָּה.
הִנֵּה הִיא יוֹרֶ֫דֶת הַקְּדוֹשָׁה הַבְּרוּכָה.
וְעִמָּהּ מַלְאָכִים צְבָא שָׁלוֹם וּמְנוּחָה.
בֹּ֫אִי בֹּ֫אִי הַמַּלְכָּה בֹּ֫אִי בֹּ֫אִי הַכַּלָּה.
שָׁלוֹם עֲלֵיכֶם מַלְאֲכֵי הַשָּׁלוֹם.

Haḥamah merosh ha'ilanot nistalekah.
Bo'u venetzey likrat shabbat hamalkah.
Hiney hi yoredet hakedoshah haberuḥah,
Ve'imah malaḥim tzeva shalom umnuḥah.
Bo'i bo'i hamalkah, bo'i bo'i hakalah.
Shalom aleyḥem malaḥey hashalom.

SHALOM ALEYḤEM

This translation can be sung to the same melody as the Hebrew.

Welcome among us, messengers of shalom,
angels of the Highest One,
from deep within us, Majesty of majesties,
the blessed Holy One.

Come, then, in shalom,
blessing us with shalom,
leaving us with holy shalom,
from deep within us, Majesty of majesties,
the blessed Holy One.

translated by Burt Jacobson

שָׁלוֹם עֲלֵיכֶם

שָׁלוֹם עֲלֵיכֶם מַלְאֲכֵי הַשָּׁרֵת מַלְאֲכֵי עֶלְיוֹן
מִמֶּֽלֶךְ מַלְכֵי הַמְּלָכִים הַקָּדוֹשׁ בָּרוּךְ הוּא:

בּוֹאֲכֶם לְשָׁלוֹם מַלְאֲכֵי הַשָּׁלוֹם מַלְאֲכֵי עֶלְיוֹן
מִמֶּֽלֶךְ מַלְכֵי הַמְּלָכִים הַקָּדוֹשׁ בָּרוּךְ הוּא:

בָּרְכֽוּנִי לְשָׁלוֹם מַלְאֲכֵי הַשָּׁלוֹם מַלְאֲכֵי עֶלְיוֹן
מִמֶּֽלֶךְ מַלְכֵי הַמְּלָכִים הַקָּדוֹשׁ בָּרוּךְ הוּא:

צֵאתְכֶם לְשָׁלוֹם מַלְאֲכֵי הַשָּׁלוֹם מַלְאֲכֵי עֶלְיוֹן
מִמֶּֽלֶךְ מַלְכֵי הַמְּלָכִים הַקָּדוֹשׁ בָּרוּךְ הוּא:

Shalom aleyḥem malaḥey hasharet malaḥey elyon
mimeleḥ malḥey hamelaḥim hakadosh baruḥ hu.

Bo'aḥem leshalom malaḥey hashalom malaḥey elyon
mimeleḥ malḥey hamelaḥim hakadosh baruḥ hu.

Bareḥuni leshalom malaḥey hashalom malaḥey elyon
mimeleḥ malḥey hamelaḥim hakadosh baruḥ hu.

Tzetḥem leshalom malaḥey hashalom malaḥey elyon
mimeleḥ malḥey hamelaḥim hakadosh baruḥ hu.

Angels are another name for feelings.
When we love and act with kindness
we create angels of love and kindness;
when we hate and act with violence
we create angels of hatred and violence.
It is our job to fill our world with angels of love:
messengers of kindness
that link people together as one family.

R.M.S.

SHIR HASHIRIM / THE SONG OF SONGS

Select from among the following:

The Song of Songs, ascribed to Solomon.

He kisses me, full kisses with his mouth.
Yes, better is your love than wine, [I say,]
Oh, the aroma of your balm!
—a balsamum poured out: your name!
For such a thing the young girls love you.
Take me along with you, let's run!

The king has brought me to his chambers:
We are gleeful, we rejoice in you, [he says,]
we bring to mind your love
  more than the finest wine,
yes, rightly they have loved you. 1:1–4

COMMENTARY. The historical origin of the love poems that comprise *Shir Hashirim* (The Song of Songs) is unknown. Were they simple shepherd love poetry, as they present themselves, or did they have a cultic setting in the distant pre-Israelite past, as some have suggested? The Kabbalists prescribed the recitation of the Song of Songs at *Kabbalat Shabbat.* They saw it as a love poem between the blessed Holy One and the *Sheḥinah,* or the male and female elements within divinity. Only in the union of these two can divine blessing flow into the world, giving us the enjoyment of Shabbat peace. A.G.

NOTE. The translator, hearing a play on words in Hebrew, uses the spice name "balsamum" because of its likeness in sound to "Solomon." King Solomon is the reputed author of *Shir Hashirim.*

שיר השירים

Select from among the following:

שִׁיר הַשִּׁירִים אֲשֶׁר לִשְׁלֹמֹה :

יִשָּׁקֵנִי מִנְּשִׁיקוֹת פִּיהוּ
כִּי־טוֹבִים דֹּדֶיךָ מִיָּיִן :
לְרֵיחַ שְׁמָנֶיךָ טוֹבִים
שֶׁמֶן תּוּרַק שְׁמֶךָ
עַל־כֵּן עֲלָמוֹת אֲהֵבוּךָ :
מָשְׁכֵנִי אַחֲרֶיךָ נָּרוּצָה

הֱבִיאַנִי הַמֶּלֶךְ חֲדָרָיו
נָגִילָה וְנִשְׂמְחָה בָּךְ
נַזְכִּירָה דֹדֶיךָ מִיַּיִן
מֵישָׁרִים אֲהֵבוּךָ :

COMMENTARY. The term *Sheḥinah* is an expansion of the biblical concept of *Kevod HaShem* כבוד ה׳, the manifest presence of God. In post-biblical literature *Sheḥinah,* which derives from the root שכן, to dwell, came to mean the feminine, in-dwelling experience of God. Jewish mystical literature elaborated this image of the *Sheḥinah* as feminine. Mystics thus saw the unity of the divine realm as dependent upon the healing union of God's transcendent (masculine) and immanent (feminine) aspects. It was believed that the people Israel can promote this healing through prayer and Torah. The rabbis understood this union between masculine and feminine, God and Israel, King and *Sheḥinah,* to be at the heart of Shir Hashirim. M.P.

I am black and lovely, daughters of Jerusalem,
like tents of faraway Kedar,
like drapes of Solomon's.
Do not be awed that I'm so swarthy,
for the sun has baked me dark.

My mother's sons have acted haughtily toward me.
They have made me sit and guard the vineyard,
but my own vineyard, my own, I have neglected.
Tell me, you whom my lifebreath loves,
where will you feed your flocks,
where will you set them down,
   at noon?
Yes, let me not be like one veiled
   among your comrades' flocks.

If you don't know, [he says,] most beautiful of women,
go forth yourself, chase on the heels
   of the departing sheep,
and feed your little lambs out by the sheepfolds.
Like a mare in Pharaoh's livery are you to me,
   my love,
your cheeks adorned with plaited wreaths,
your neck with beaded cords.
Some golden wreaths we'll make for you,
   with silvered points.

While the king is on his loveseat,
my meadowgrass gives forth its scent.
As lovely as a myrrh sachet my lover is to me,
he'll spend the night between my breasts.
Like henna clusters in the vineyards
   of En-Gedi is my love to me.

שְׁחוֹרָה אֲנִי וְנָאוָה בְּנוֹת יְרוּשָׁלָיִם
כְּאָהֳלֵי קֵדָר
כִּירִיעוֹת שְׁלֹמֹה׃
אַל־תִּרְאֻנִי שֶׁאֲנִי שְׁחַרְחֹרֶת
שֶׁשְּׁזָפַתְנִי הַשָּׁמֶשׁ

בְּנֵי אִמִּי נִחֲרוּ־בִי
שָׂמֻנִי נֹטֵרָה אֶת־הַכְּרָמִים
כַּרְמִי שֶׁלִּי לֹא נָטָרְתִּי׃
הַגִּידָה לִּי שֶׁאָהֲבָה נַפְשִׁי
אֵיכָה תִרְעֶה
אֵיכָה תַּרְבִּיץ בַּצָּהֳרָיִם
שַׁלָּמָה אֶהְיֶה כְּעֹטְיָה עַל עֶדְרֵי חֲבֵרֶיךָ׃

אִם־לֹא תֵדְעִי לָךְ הַיָּפָה בַּנָּשִׁים
צְאִי־לָךְ בְּעִקְבֵי הַצֹּאן
וּרְעִי אֶת־גְּדִיֹּתַיִךְ עַל מִשְׁכְּנוֹת הָרֹעִים׃
לְסֻסָתִי בְּרִכְבֵי פַרְעֹה דִּמִּיתִיךְ רַעְיָתִי׃
נָאווּ לְחָיַיִךְ בַּתֹּרִים
צַוָּארֵךְ בַּחֲרוּזִים׃
תּוֹרֵי זָהָב נַעֲשֶׂה־לָּךְ עִם נְקֻדּוֹת הַכָּסֶף׃

עַד־שֶׁהַמֶּלֶךְ בִּמְסִבּוֹ
נִרְדִּי נָתַן רֵיחוֹ׃
צְרוֹר הַמֹּר ׀ דּוֹדִי לִי
בֵּין שָׁדַי יָלִין׃
אֶשְׁכֹּל הַכֹּפֶר ׀ דּוֹדִי לִי בְּכַרְמֵי עֵין גֶּדִי׃ ←

Here you are, so beautiful, my friend, [he says].
Why, here you are, so beautiful,
your eyes like doves, yes,
here you are, so beautiful, my love,
and oh, how much delight,
and oh, how fresh our bed!
Our house's roofbeams are of cedar,
and the rafters made of cypress wood. 1:5–17

I am a rose of Sharon, [I say,]
a lily of the valley.

Like a lily among thorns, [he says,]
so is my love among young women.

Like an apple in the forest's trees,
[I say,] so is my love among young men.

And I grow moist just sitting in his shadow,
with his fruit so sweet against my palate.

He has brought me to the house of wines,
his love-banner unfurled above me.

O, give me sun-dried fruit for strength,
oh, wake me from my swoon with apples,
yes, for I grow faint with love!

His left hand reaches down behind my head,
and with his right hand he caresses me.

הִנָּ֤ךְ יָפָה֙ רַעְיָתִ֔י
הִנָּ֥ךְ יָפָ֖ה
עֵינַ֥יִךְ יוֹנִֽים :
הִנְּךָ֨ יָפֶ֤ה דוֹדִי֙
אַ֣ף נָעִ֔ים
אַף־עַרְשֵׂ֖נוּ רַעֲנָנָֽה :
קֹר֤וֹת בָּתֵּ֙ינוּ֙ אֲרָזִ֔ים רָהִיטֵ֖נוּ בְּרוֹתִֽים :

1:5–17

אֲנִי֙ חֲבַצֶּ֣לֶת הַשָּׁר֔וֹן
שֽׁוֹשַׁנַּ֖ת הָעֲמָקִֽים :

כְּשֽׁוֹשַׁנָּה֙ בֵּ֣ין הַחוֹחִ֔ים
כֵּ֥ן רַעְיָתִ֖י בֵּ֥ין הַבָּנֽוֹת :

כְּתַפּ֙וּחַ֙ בַּעֲצֵ֣י הַיַּ֔עַר
כֵּ֥ן דוֹדִ֖י בֵּ֣ין הַבָּנִ֑ים

בְּצִלּוֹ֙ חִמַּ֣דְתִּי וְיָשַׁ֔בְתִּי
וּפִרְי֖וֹ מָת֥וֹק לְחִכִּֽי :

הֱבִיאַ֙נִי֙ אֶל־בֵּ֣ית הַיָּ֔יִן
וְדִגְל֥וֹ עָלַ֖י אַהֲבָֽה :

סַמְּכ֙וּנִי֙ בָּֽאֲשִׁישׁ֔וֹת
רַפְּד֖וּנִי בַּתַּפּוּחִ֑ים
כִּי־חוֹלַ֥ת אַהֲבָ֖ה אָֽנִי :

שְׂמֹאלוֹ֙ תַּ֣חַת לְרֹאשִׁ֔י
וִימִינ֖וֹ תְּחַבְּקֵֽנִי : ←

Oh, I adjure you, daughters of Jerusalem,
by the gazelles and by the hinds out on the field,

do not stir up, do not awaken love,
till it can please.

The voice of my beloved—look, he's coming
dancing on the mountains, leaping on the hills.

My love is like a hart,
yes, like a stag of the gazelles.

Look at him standing there behind our wall,
inspecting through the window,
gazing through the latticework. 2:1–9

My love called out to me, and said:
"Rise up, dear mate, my lovely one,
and come forth. Look! The chill has fled.
The rain has passed, has gone its way,
and blossoms have appeared upon the land.
The pruning time has come,
and chortling doves are heard around our land.
The figs have livened up their hue,
the vines have given forth their fruit's bouquet.
Rise up, dear mate, my lovely one,
come out! My dove, you who are nestled
in the cranny of the rock,
in the hollow of the step's ascent,
show me your form, and let me hear your voice,
for oh, how sweet your voice,
and oh, how fine your form!
Go catch us foxes, little foxes,
vineyard wreckers, in our fruit-filled vineyard!" ↩

הִשְׁבַּ֨עְתִּי אֶתְכֶ֜ם בְּנ֣וֹת יְרוּשָׁלַ֗͏ִם
בִּצְבָא֔וֹת א֖וֹ בְּאַיְל֣וֹת הַשָּׂדֶ֑ה

אִם־תָּעִ֧ירוּ ׀ וְֽאִם־תְּעֽוֹרְר֛וּ אֶת־הָאַהֲבָ֖ה עַ֥ד שֶׁתֶּחְפָּֽץ׃

ק֤וֹל דּוֹדִי֙ הִנֵּה־זֶ֣ה בָּ֔א
מְדַלֵּג֙ עַל־הֶ֣הָרִ֔ים מְקַפֵּ֖ץ עַל־הַגְּבָעֽוֹת׃

דּוֹמֶ֤ה דוֹדִי֙ לִצְבִ֔י א֖וֹ לְעֹ֣פֶר הָֽאַיָּלִ֑ים

הִנֵּה־זֶה֙ עוֹמֵד֙ אַחַ֣ר כָּתְלֵ֔נוּ
מַשְׁגִּ֙יחַ֙ מִן־הַֽחַלֹּנ֔וֹת מֵצִ֖יץ מִן־הַֽחֲרַכִּֽים׃

Kol dodi hiney zeh ba
medaleg al heharim
mekapetz al hageva'ot.

2:1–9

עָנָ֥ה דוֹדִ֖י וְאָ֣מַר לִ֑י ק֥וּמִי לָ֛ךְ רַעְיָתִ֥י יָפָתִ֖י
וּלְכִי־לָֽךְ׃ כִּֽי־הִנֵּ֥ה הַסְּתָ֖ו עָבָ֑ר
הַגֶּ֕שֶׁם חָלַ֖ף הָלַ֥ךְ לֽוֹ׃ הַנִּצָּנִים֙ נִרְא֣וּ בָאָ֔רֶץ
עֵ֥ת הַזָּמִ֖יר הִגִּ֑יעַ וְק֥וֹל הַתּ֖וֹר נִשְׁמַ֥ע בְּאַרְצֵֽנוּ׃
הַתְּאֵנָה֙ חָֽנְטָ֣ה פַגֶּ֔יהָ
וְהַגְּפָנִ֥ים ׀ סְמָדַ֖ר נָ֣תְנוּ רֵ֑יחַ
ק֥וּמִי לָ֛ךְ רַעְיָתִ֥י יָפָתִ֖י
וּלְכִי־לָֽךְ׃ יוֹנָתִ֞י
בְּחַגְוֵ֣י הַסֶּ֗לַע בְּסֵ֙תֶר֙ הַמַּדְרֵגָ֔ה
הַרְאִ֙ינִי֙ אֶת־מַרְאַ֔יִךְ הַשְׁמִיעִ֖ינִי אֶת־קוֹלֵ֑ךְ
כִּֽי־קוֹלֵ֥ךְ עָרֵ֖ב וּמַרְאֵ֥יךְ נָאוֶֽה׃
אֶחֱזוּ־לָ֙נוּ֙ שֻֽׁעָלִ֔ים שֻׁעָלִ֥ים קְטַנִּ֖ים
מְחַבְּלִ֣ים כְּרָמִ֑ים וּכְרָמֵ֖ינוּ סְמָדַֽר׃ ⟶

"My love is mine, and I am his,
who browses in the lotus patch.
Before the day has breathed its last
and shadows have all fled,
come 'round and strike a pose, my love,
of a gazelle, or of a young buck
of the rams, out on a mountain cleft." 2:10–17

"Come forth from Lebanon, my bride,
come forth from Lebanon, yes, come!
Appear upon Amana's crest,
or from Senir's or Hermon's peak,
or from the lion's lairs,
or from the panther's heights.

You have enlivened me, my sister-bride,
you have enlivened me with but a single glance,
with just a glinting of your neckpiece.
How beautiful your love, my sister-bride,
how beautiful your love, finer than wine!
Your smell's aroma, finer than all spices,
lips dewy with honeycomb. O bride!
Honey and milk beneath your tongue,
your seemly shawl smelling of Lebanon,

דּוֹדִי לִי֙ וַאֲנִ֣י ל֔וֹ
הָרֹעֶ֖ה בַּשּׁוֹשַׁנִּֽים׃
עַ֤ד שֶׁיָּפ֙וּחַ֙ הַיּ֔וֹם
וְנָ֖סוּ הַצְּלָלִ֑ים
סֹב֩ דְּמֵה־לְךָ֨ דוֹדִ֜י
לִצְבִ֗י א֛וֹ לְעֹ֥פֶר הָאַיָּלִ֖ים
עַל־הָ֥רֵי בָֽתֶר׃

Dodi li va'ani lo haro'eh bashoshanim.

2:10–17

אִתִּ֤י מִלְּבָנוֹן֙ כַּלָּ֔ה
אִתִּ֖י מִלְּבָנ֣וֹן תָּב֑וֹאִי
תָּשׁ֣וּרִי ׀ מֵרֹ֣אשׁ אֲמָנָ֗ה
מֵרֹ֤אשׁ שְׂנִיר֙ וְחֶרְמ֔וֹן
מִמְּעֹנ֣וֹת אֲרָי֔וֹת
מֵהַֽרְרֵ֖י נְמֵרִֽים׃

לִבַּבְתִּ֖נִי אֲחֹתִ֣י כַלָּ֑ה
לִבַּבְתִּ֙נִי֙ בְּאַחַ֣ת מֵעֵינַ֔יִךְ
בְּאַחַ֥ד עֲנָ֖ק מִצַּוְּרֹנָֽיִךְ׃
מַה־יָּפ֥וּ דֹדַ֖יִךְ אֲחֹתִ֣י כַלָּ֑ה
מַה־טֹּ֤בוּ דֹדַ֙יִךְ֙ מִיַּ֔יִן
וְרֵ֥יחַ שְׁמָנַ֖יִךְ מִכָּל־בְּשָׂמִֽים׃
נֹ֛פֶת תִּטֹּ֥פְנָה שִׂפְתוֹתַ֖יִךְ כַּלָּ֑ה
דְּבַ֤שׁ וְחָלָב֙ תַּ֣חַת לְשׁוֹנֵ֔ךְ
וְרֵ֥יחַ שַׂלְמֹתַ֖יִךְ כְּרֵ֥יחַ לְבָנֽוֹן׃ ←

Libavtini aḥoti ḥalah.

a sealed-up garden is my sister-bride,
a swell enclosed, a sheltered fount.
Your crevices, a pomegranate orchard,
with the finest blossomings: here
cypresses with meadowgrass;
yes, meadowgrass and saffron,
cane and cinnamon, with all the woods
of olibanum, myrrh, and aloes,
and the choicest spices.

A garden spring, a well of living waters,
flowing down from Lebanon."
"Awake, north wind,
yes, come, south wind! Blow on my garden,
let its spices flow. Let my love come
to see his garden, and to eat
of its exquisite fruits." 4:8–16

COMMENTARY. Jewish sources have understood *Shir Hashirim* as a love dialogue between the community of Israel and its God. According to midrash,* Israel is the beautiful dark servant-girl coming forth from the wilderness after she is redeemed from Egypt. She and her divine lover seek one another, whisper terms of endearment, call out in voices of longing, and rejoice as they approach their sacred union. To Rabbi Akiva is attributed the astonishing assertion, "All of Scripture is holy, but the Song of Songs is the Holy of Holies!" A.G.

לבונה. The translator has used the spice name "olibanum" to reflect a play on words between *levonah* and *levanon*/Lebanon. Olibanum is also known as frankincense.

גַּ֣ן ׀ נָע֑וּל אֲחֹתִ֣י כַלָּ֔ה
גַּ֥ל נָע֖וּל מַעְיָ֥ן חָת֛וּם׃
שְׁלָחַ֙יִךְ֙ פַּרְדֵּ֣ס רִמּוֹנִ֔ים
עִ֖ם פְּרִ֣י מְגָדִ֑ים כְּפָרִ֖ים עִם־נְרָדִֽים׃
נֵ֣רְדְּ ׀ וְכַרְכֹּ֗ם קָנֶה֙ וְקִנָּמ֔וֹן
עִ֖ם כָּל־עֲצֵ֣י לְבוֹנָ֑ה מֹ֚ר וַאֲהָל֔וֹת
עִ֖ם כָּל־רָאשֵׁ֥י בְשָׂמִֽים׃

מַעְיַ֣ן גַּנִּ֔ים בְּאֵ֖ר מַ֣יִם חַיִּ֑ים
וְנֹזְלִ֖ים מִן־לְבָנֽוֹן׃

ע֤וּרִי צָפוֹן֙ וּב֣וֹאִי תֵימָ֔ן הָפִ֥יחִי גַנִּ֖י
יִזְּל֣וּ בְשָׂמָ֑יו יָבֹ֤א דוֹדִי֙
לְגַנּ֔וֹ וְיֹאכַ֖ל פְּרִ֥י מְגָדָֽיו׃

Uri tzafon uvo'i teyman.

4:8–16

DERASH. One may read the Song of Songs as a poem reconciling disparate, often polarized aspects of each human soul. Shelomo and Shulamit (whose names mean peace and wholeness) are symbols of unification. We must not hide from light our darkest, most passionate, most aroused and sensual parts. Male and female, maiden and royalty, palace and field, blossom and fruit, animals, birds and plants all draw into harmony on this day of inclusive, overflowing love and self-acceptance.

S.P.W.

*Midrash is a genre of interpretative commentary that derives its name from the root דרש: to seek or search out. The activity of expounding midrash is one of elucidation through creative expansion of words, verses, or whole stories that are ambiguous in the biblical text. These provide fertile ground for imaginative explanation. Midrashic literature dates back to the period of the early Amoraic rabbis, ca. 400 C.E., and is still being created today.

M.P.

PSALMS

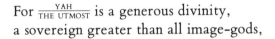

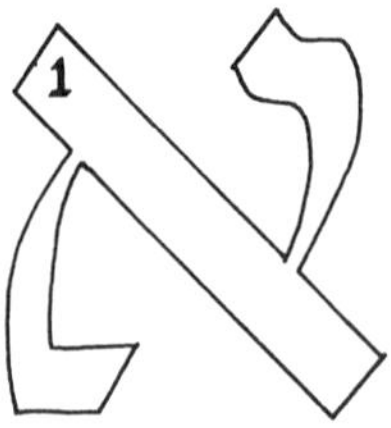

Psalm 95

Come, sing in ecstasy to YAH / CELESTIAL
ring out a fanfare to our rock of rescue!

Hurry forth in thanks before the Presence,
shouting in song to God.

For YAH / THE UTMOST is a generous divinity,
a sovereign greater than all image-gods,

in whose hand the planetary depths reside,
the greatest heights, there in God's palm,

to whom belongs the sea, as it was made,
the dry land, shaped by divine hand.

Come worship, bend the knee,
let's bow to YAH / THE EMINENCE who made us all.

COMMENTARY. The five psalms of *Kabbalat Shabbat,* Psalms 95–99, are a literary unit within the Book of Psalms. Their spirit of joy and exultation calls on the worshipper to rejoice in the presence of God that fills the world. Nature itself joins in the symphony of praise as heaven and earth, field and forest, sea and rivers all seem to clap hands and enter the song and dance of joy. The coming of Shabbat fills us with a new vision, one that sees earth as freshly created and brimming with divine radiance. This vision is a universal one. It invites all nations to join in our celebration of divine presence. A.G.

לְכוּ נְרַנְּנָה לַיהוה נָרִֽיעָה לְצוּר יִשְׁעֵֽנוּ׃
נְקַדְּמָה פָנָיו בְּתוֹדָה בִּזְמִרוֹת נָרִֽיעַ לוֹ׃
כִּי אֵל גָּדוֹל יהוה וּמֶֽלֶךְ גָּדוֹל עַל־כָּל־אֱלֹהִים׃
אֲשֶׁר בְּיָדוֹ מֶחְקְרֵי־אָֽרֶץ וְתוֹעֲפוֹת הָרִים לוֹ׃
אֲשֶׁר־לוֹ הַיָּם וְהוּא עָשָׂהוּ וְיַבֶּֽשֶׁת יָדָיו יָצָֽרוּ׃
בֹּֽאוּ נִשְׁתַּחֲוֶה וְנִכְרָֽעָה נִבְרְכָה לִפְנֵי־יהוה עֹשֵֽׂנוּ׃ ⟵

Leḥu neranenah ladonay nari'ah letzur yishenu.
Nekademah fanav betodah bizmirot nari'ah lo.
Ki el gadol adonay umeleḥ gadol al kol elohim.
Asher beyado meḥkerey aretz veto'afot harim lo.

COMMENTARY. It may be the concluding line of Psalm 95 that caused this entire group of psalms to be included in *Kabbalat Shabbat.* The psalmist speaks of the forty years in the wilderness, saying that the generation who came out of Egypt were not able "to enter God's place of rest," the Holy Land promised at the end of Israel's wanderings. But here in *Kabbalat Shabbat* "rest" has taken on a new meaning; it is in *time* rather than in *place* that rest is to be found. Shabbat has itself become a Holy Land, a time of rest in which we are called upon to cease our wandering. A.G.

This is our God,
and we, nurtured by God, a flock under God's care

—today:
if to the Voice
you'll listen—:

"Harden not your heart as it was done at Meribah,
as on a day of trial in the wilderness,

there your predecessors tested me,
they put to trial my patience, but they saw my power.

For forty years I argued with that generation,
till finally I said: 'They are a people with a wandering heart,'

nor did they ever
come to know
my ways.

And as for them, I swore amid my wrath,
that they'll not come into my place of rest."

כִּי הוּא אֱלֹהֵינוּ   וַאֲנַחְנוּ עַם מַרְעִיתוֹ וְצֹאן יָדוֹ
הַיּוֹם אִם־בְּקֹלוֹ תִשְׁמָעוּ:

אַל־תַּקְשׁוּ לְבַבְכֶם כִּמְרִיבָה   כְּיוֹם מַסָּה בַּמִּדְבָּר:
אֲשֶׁר נִסּוּנִי אֲבוֹתֵיכֶם   בְּחָנוּנִי גַּם־רָאוּ פָעֳלִי:
אַרְבָּעִים שָׁנָה אָקוּט בְּדוֹר   וָאֹמַר עַם תֹּעֵי לֵבָב הֵם
וְהֵם לֹא־יָדְעוּ דְרָכָי:

אֲשֶׁר נִשְׁבַּעְתִּי בְאַפִּי   אִם־יְבֹאוּן אֶל־מְנוּחָתִי:

DERASH. The ancients deemed obedience to God's will to be a prime virtue. Abraham had it; Adam lacked it. In our own day this virtue must mean the power to conform to the basic law of life. Obedience to that law brings salvation; defiance of it leads to disaster. M.M.K. (ADAPTED)

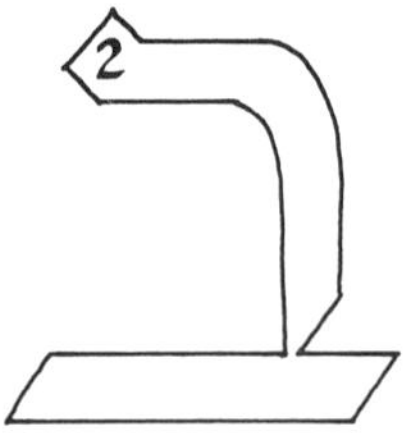

Psalm 96

Sing out to YAH/THE IMAGELESS a new song!
Sing to YAH/THE SOURCE all the earth!

Sing to YAH/THE SUBLIME ONE—bless God's name,
Bring news, day after day, of divine help.

Tell it among the nations, tell the glory,
among all the peoples, tell of miracles.

Yes, YAH/THE RADIANCE is great, subject of praise indeed,
the source of awe, above all image-gods!

For all the nation-gods are idols,
but YAH/THE LIVING ONE has made the heavens.

Grandeur and splendor belong to God,
Strength and beauty in the Holy Place.

Give praise to YAH/THE MAGNIFICENT families of nations,
Honor and power devote to YAH/THE AWESOME ONE.

Pay homage to YAH/MAJESTY for the glory of the name.
bear offering, approach the Courtyards,

bow down to YAH/GRANDEUR with holy adornment,
tremble in God's presence, all the earth.

Declare among the nations that YAH/THE ESSENCE reigns;
the world is founded, none can topple it;

the peoples
shall be judged
unerringly.

שִׁירוּ לַיהוה שִׁיר חָדָשׁ שִׁירוּ לַיהוה כׇּל־הָאָרֶץ׃
שִׁירוּ לַיהוה בָּרְכוּ שְׁמוֹ בַּשְּׂרוּ מִיּוֹם לְיוֹם יְשׁוּעָתוֹ׃
סַפְּרוּ בַגּוֹיִם כְּבוֹדוֹ בְּכׇל־הָעַמִּים נִפְלְאוֹתָיו׃
כִּי גָדוֹל יהוה וּמְהֻלָּל מְאֹד נוֹרָא הוּא עַל־כׇּל־אֱלֹהִים׃
כִּי כׇּל־אֱלֹהֵי הָעַמִּים אֱלִילִים וַיהוה שָׁמַיִם עָשָׂה׃
הוֹד־וְהָדָר לְפָנָיו עֹז וְתִפְאֶרֶת בְּמִקְדָּשׁוֹ׃
הָבוּ לַיהוה מִשְׁפְּחוֹת עַמִּים הָבוּ לַיהוה כָּבוֹד וָעֹז׃
הָבוּ לַיהוה כְּבוֹד שְׁמוֹ שְׂאוּ מִנְחָה וּבֹאוּ לְחַצְרוֹתָיו׃
הִשְׁתַּחֲווּ לַיהוה בְּהַדְרַת־קֹדֶשׁ חִילוּ מִפָּנָיו כׇּל־הָאָרֶץ׃
אִמְרוּ בַגּוֹיִם יהוה מָלָךְ אַף־תִּכּוֹן תֵּבֵל בַּל־תִּמּוֹט
יָדִין עַמִּים בְּמֵישָׁרִים׃ ←

Shiru ladonay shir ḥadash, shiru ladonay kol ha'aretz.
Shiru ladonay bareḥu shemo, baseru miyom leyom yeshu'ato.
Saperu vagoyim kevodo, beḥol ha'amim nifle'otav.
Ki gadol adonay umhulal me'od, no-ra hu al kol elohim.
Ki kol elohey ha'amim elilim, vadonay shamayim asah.
Hod vehadar lefanav, oz vetiferet bemikdasho.
Havu ladonay mishpeḥot amim, havu ladonay kavod va'oz.
Havu ladonay kevod shemo, se'u minḥah uvo'u leḥatzrotav.
Hishtaḥavu ladonay behadrat kodesh, ḥilu mipanav kol ha'aretz.
Imru vagoyim adonay malaḥ, af tikon tevel bal timot.
Yadin amim bemeysharim. ↩

תכון תבל / the world is founded. There is cosmic order. L.W.K.

Let the skies rejoice, the earth have glee.
Ocean resound, in all your fullness!

Let the fields rejoice, and all belonging there.
And then, all forest trees exclaim ecstatically,

before YAH / THE ONE who comes,
who comes to rule the earth,

to rule over the settled world,
over the peoples, faithfully.

DERASH. This psalm makes no explicit reference to Israel, Jews, or Judaism. All nations, all forces are controlled by God.

The psalmist shouts: יהוה is great—every day, always, everywhere, to everybody; come, join me in praising! The writer knows of the greatness of God from experience, not reason. The presence of God reaches beyond one person, beyond a nation, beyond human beings!

This great God makes demands on us; we are accountable for our actions. God judges; we must act justly. L.W.K.

KAVANAH. To affirm the sovereignty of God means to acknowledge a higher law and authority than one's own arbitrary will. M.M.K.

יִשְׂמְחוּ הַשָּׁמַיִם וְתָגֵל הָאָרֶץ יִרְעַם הַיָּם וּמְלֹאוֹ׃
יַעֲלֹז שָׂדַי וְכָל־אֲשֶׁר־בּוֹ אָז יְרַנְּנוּ כָּל־עֲצֵי־יָעַר׃
לִפְנֵי יהוה כִּי בָא כִּי בָא לִשְׁפֹּט הָאָרֶץ
יִשְׁפֹּט־תֵּבֵל בְּצֶדֶק וְעַמִּים בֶּאֱמוּנָתוֹ׃

Yismeḥu hashamayim vetagel ha'aretz yiram hayam umlo'o.
Ya'aloz saday veḥol asher bo, az yeranenu kol atzey ya'ar.
Lifney adonay ki va, ki va lishpot ha'aretz.
Yishpot tevel betzedek, ve'amim be'emunato.

באמונתו / *be'emunato:* faithfully; **אמונה** / *emunah* means trust, constancy, or rightness. **בצדק**, **במישרים**, **באמונתו** form a triplet stressing the justice and fairness of **יהוה**. L.W.K.

Psalm 97

YAH/THE UNCREATED reigns! O world, rejoice!
Be happy, dwellers of all continents!

Clouds and thick darkness surround God,
justice and judgment bear up the Throne,

a fire goes before it,
flames surround its back,

its lightning flashes light the world,
the earth beholds and trembles,

mountains melt like wax before YAH/THE ONE
before the First of all the earth,

whose justice all the skies declare,
whose glory all the nations see.

Let all who worship images be shamed,
all those who boast amid their idols,

let all gods
submit
to God.

Zion has heard, and has rejoiced,
the women of Judah sound their joy,

because of justice,
yours
YAH/BRIGHT ONE •

יהוה מָלָךְ תָּגֵל הָאָֽרֶץ יִשְׂמְחוּ אִיִּים רַבִּים׃
עָנָן וַעֲרָפֶל סְבִיבָיו צֶֽדֶק וּמִשְׁפָּט מְכוֹן כִּסְאוֹ׃
אֵשׁ לְפָנָיו תֵּלֵךְ וּתְלַהֵט סָבִיב צָרָיו׃
הֵאִֽירוּ בְרָקָיו תֵּבֵל רָאֲתָה וַתָּֽחֵל הָאָֽרֶץ׃
הָרִים כַּדּוֹנַג נָמַֽסּוּ מִלִּפְנֵי יהוה מִלִּפְנֵי אֲדוֹן כׇּל־הָאָֽרֶץ׃
הִגִּֽידוּ הַשָּׁמַֽיִם צִדְקוֹ וְרָאוּ כׇל־הָעַמִּים כְּבוֹדוֹ׃
יֵבֹֽשׁוּ כׇּל־עֹֽבְדֵי פֶֽסֶל הַמִּתְהַלְלִים בָּאֱלִילִים
הִשְׁתַּחֲווּ־לוֹ כׇּל־אֱלֹהִים׃

שָֽׁמְעָה וַתִּשְׂמַח צִיּוֹן וַתָּגֵֽלְנָה בְּנוֹת יְהוּדָה
לְמַֽעַן מִשְׁפָּטֶֽיךָ יהוה׃ ⟵

KAVANAH. The belief in the sovereignty of God should keep in our minds the prophetic teaching that God should be obeyed rather than worshipped, that obedience to God's laws is the highest form of worship. It is an error to believe that the main function of the spiritual is to afford us an escape from the turmoil and the temptations of life—a sort of ivory tower of detachment. The truth of the sovereignty of God should remind us that our task is to turn temptations into a means of serving God.

M.M.K. (ADAPTED)

בנות יהודה/Judea's daughters, the women of Judah. The place rejoices, then the people join in. Some say that "daughters" includes the place itself.

L.W.K.

For you are $\frac{\text{YAH}}{\text{THE RADIANCE}}$
above all earth.

Powerfully, you have ascended
over all the image-gods.

And you who love $\frac{\text{YAH}}{\text{THE GREAT ONE}}$ hate the bad,
so that the Guardian of loving souls

might save them
from the power
of the wicked.

Lightbeams are seeded for the righteous,
Happiness for those steadfast of heart,

Rejoice, O righteous ones in $\frac{\text{YAH}}{\text{THE UNNAMEABLE}}$
be thankful for its sacred Trace!

כִּי־אַתָּה יהוה עֶלְיוֹן עַל־כָּל־הָאָרֶץ
מְאֹד נַעֲלֵיתָ עַל־כָּל־אֱלֹהִים׃
אֹהֲבֵי יהוה שִׂנְאוּ רָע שֹׁמֵר נַפְשׁוֹת חֲסִידָיו
מִיַּד רְשָׁעִים יַצִּילֵם׃

אוֹר זָרֻעַ לַצַּדִּיק וּלְיִשְׁרֵי־לֵב שִׂמְחָה׃
שִׂמְחוּ צַדִּיקִים בַּיהוה וְהוֹדוּ לְזֵכֶר קָדְשׁוֹ׃

Or zaru'a latzadik, ulyishrey lev simḥah.
Simḥu tzadikim badonay vehodu lezeḥer kodsho.

. . . אוהבי / you who love. . . . The lover of God naturally fights evil. Ethics and spirituality are closely linked.

שמר נפשות / God protects. Those who fight injustice are often in need of protection.

זרוע / seeded. Light is like seeds because it needs to be nourished and tended. It demands patience. Another reading is זרוח / *zaru'aḥ,* a brilliant, dazzling light (The Me'iri).

לישרי לב / right-hearted, steadfast of heart—those with focused minds.

L.W.K.

4 Psalm 98

A psalm: Sing out to YAH/THE TRUTHFUL a new song,
to One who has wrought wonders in the world,

whose right hand was of aid,
as was the holy, saving arm,

who made the divine might renowned,
revealed God's justice to the eyes of many nations,

and who made remembered divine love and faithfulness
to the community of Israel.

To the farthest reaches of the earth, they saw
our God's salvation!

Trumpet out in joy to YAH/THE AWESOME ONE's praise,
burst forth and sing, and play your music,

music for YAH/THE OMNIPRESENT on a violin,
on strings, with voice and melody,

with hornplaying and shofar blasts,
trumpet your praise before the sovereign, to YAH/THE ONE WHO IS!

Let the sea be in a tumult,
and the settled world, and its inhabitants.

And let the rivers clap their hands
together, and the mountains sing in joy,

to YAH/THE ONE who comes to rule the earth,

to rule the settled world with justice,
and all peoples with unerring deeds!

מִזְמוֹר

שִׁירוּ לַיהוה שִׁיר חָדָשׁ כִּי־נִפְלָאוֹת עָשָׂה

הוֹשִׁיעָה־לּוֹ יְמִינוֹ וּזְרוֹעַ קָדְשׁוֹ׃

הוֹדִיעַ יהוה יְשׁוּעָתוֹ לְעֵינֵי הַגּוֹיִם גִּלָּה צִדְקָתוֹ׃

זָכַר חַסְדּוֹ וֶאֱמוּנָתוֹ לְבֵית יִשְׂרָאֵל

רָאוּ כָל־אַפְסֵי־אָרֶץ אֵת יְשׁוּעַת אֱלֹהֵינוּ׃

הָרִיעוּ לַיהוה כָּל־הָאָרֶץ פִּצְחוּ וְרַנְּנוּ וְזַמֵּרוּ׃

זַמְּרוּ לַיהוה בְּכִנּוֹר בְּכִנּוֹר וְקוֹל זִמְרָה׃

בַּחֲצֹצְרוֹת וְקוֹל שׁוֹפָר הָרִיעוּ לִפְנֵי הַמֶּלֶךְ יהוה׃

יִרְעַם הַיָּם וּמְלֹאוֹ תֵּבֵל וְיֹשְׁבֵי בָהּ׃

נְהָרוֹת יִמְחֲאוּ־כָף יַחַד הָרִים יְרַנֵּנוּ׃

לִפְנֵי יהוה כִּי בָא לִשְׁפֹּט הָאָרֶץ יִשְׁפֹּט תֵּבֵל בְּצֶדֶק

וְעַמִּים בְּמֵישָׁרִים׃

זכר / *zaḥar:* has been loving; literally, remembers his love. The verb is related to זכר, potent; it implies acting on the memory. L.W.K.

DERASH. One of the fundamental implications of the sovereignty of God is that religion must be socialized. It must be translated into terms of social righteousness and not stop at the inward peace and serenity of the individual. M.M.K. (ADAPTED)

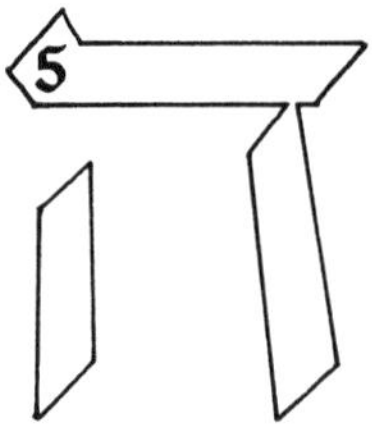

Psalm 99

YAH / THE ONE OF SINAI reigns, as nations seethe,
and sits between the cherubim, the earth is teetering.

YAH / THE ONE WHO DWELLS IN ZION is magnificent,
high above all peoples;

let them thank your name, so great and awesome,
holy it is!

With royal strength, but loving justice,
you have established equitable deeds.

Justice and righteousness on Jacob's behalf
have you performed.

Exalt YAH / THE ONE WHO SEES our God,
bow down before God's footstool,

God is holy!

Moses and Aaron are among God's priests,
and Samuel among the ones who call God's name,

Calling to YAH / THE RIGHTEOUS ONE
who will respond to them.

In a cloud pillar, God speaks to them,
they keep God's precepts and God gives them rulings.

YAH / GREAT ONE you have answered them,
you were a forgiving God for them,

after you exacted penalty for things they did.

Exalt the name of YAH / THE INEFFABLE ONE,
bow down before the sacred divine mount,

yes, holy is YAH / THE AWESOME ONE our God!

יהוה מָלָךְ יִרְגְּזוּ עַמִּים   יֹשֵׁב כְּרוּבִים תָּנוּט הָאָרֶץ׃
יהוה בְּצִיּוֹן גָּדוֹל   וְרָם הוּא עַל־כׇּל־הָעַמִּים׃
יוֹדוּ שִׁמְךָ גָּדוֹל וְנוֹרָא   קָדוֹשׁ הוּא׃
וְעֹז מֶלֶךְ מִשְׁפָּט אָהֵב   אַתָּה כּוֹנַנְתָּ מֵישָׁרִים
מִשְׁפָּט וּצְדָקָה בְּיַעֲקֹב   אַתָּה עָשִׂיתָ׃
רוֹמְמוּ יהוה אֱלֹהֵינוּ   וְהִשְׁתַּחֲווּ לַהֲדֹם רַגְלָיו
קָדוֹשׁ הוּא׃

מֹשֶׁה וְאַהֲרֹן בְּכֹהֲנָיו   וּשְׁמוּאֵל בְּקֹרְאֵי שְׁמוֹ
קֹרְאִים אֶל־יהוה   וְהוּא יַעֲנֵם׃
בְּעַמּוּד עָנָן יְדַבֵּר אֲלֵיהֶם   שָׁמְרוּ עֵדֹתָיו וְחֹק נָתַן־לָמוֹ׃
יהוה אֱלֹהֵינוּ אַתָּה עֲנִיתָם   אֵל נֹשֵׂא הָיִיתָ לָהֶם
וְנֹקֵם עַל־עֲלִילוֹתָם׃

רוֹמְמוּ יהוה אֱלֹהֵינוּ   וְהִשְׁתַּחֲווּ לְהַר קׇדְשׁוֹ
כִּי־קָדוֹשׁ יהוה אֱלֹהֵינוּ׃

הדם רגליו / footstool—the Ark, which contained the tablets of the covenant (the Ten Commandments). In the ancient Near East, international contracts were kept under the ruler's throne.

בעמוד ענן / pillar of mist, cloud or smoke, perhaps of incense. A symbol for the mystery of how the human and divine speak to each other.

אל נשא / forgiving God (from נשא, to carry), "who puts up with." Even Moses, Miriam, and Samuel made mistakes and needed forgiveness.

L.W.K.

ו 6 Psalm 29

A psalm of David: Give to YAH / THE ONE WHO IS you so-called gods,
give to YAH / THE INDIVISIBLE glory and strength!

Give to YAH / THE UNSEEN ONE the glory of the divine Name,
worship YAH / THE ANCIENT OF DAYS with holy ornament.

The voice of YAH / THE UNENDING on the waters,
God in full Glory thundering,

YAH / THE ONE WHO CALLS over many waters,

yes, voice of YAH / THE REVEALED ONE in full strength,
voice of YAH / THE TRUTHFUL in full beauty,

voice of YAH / ETERNAL LAW breaking the cedars,
YAH / THE ALL-KNOWING smashing cedar forests on Mt. Lebanon,

making them skip about like calves,
yes, Lebanon and Sirion, like offspring of the wild ox.

COMMENTARY. Psalm 29, one of the most ancient in the Book of Psalms, celebrates the presence of God in the midst of a great thunderstorm. The word *kol,* which appears seven times in the psalm, here translated "voice," can also mean "thunderclap." The psalmist concludes with mention of a great quiet that follows the storm, recalling the mythic quiet that followed God's triumph over the forces of chaos in Creation. The placing of the psalm here reminds us that our weekly struggle in the world of achievement and bustle is now at an end. We have repeated the struggles of creation and now we too are called upon to achieve that great inner quiet which is the secret of true rest. A.G.

NOTE. In this psalm the divine name, יהוה, appears eighteen times. The translator has rendered thirteen of these to recall thirteen divine attributes, and the remaining five to echo the themes of the Five Books of Moses.

מִזְמוֹר לְדָוִד
הָבוּ לַיהוה בְּנֵי אֵלִים הָבוּ לַיהוה כָּבוֹד וָעֹז׃
הָבוּ לַיהוה כְּבוֹד שְׁמוֹ הִשְׁתַּחֲווּ לַיהוה בְּהַדְרַת־קֹֽדֶשׁ׃
קוֹל יהוה עַל־הַמָּֽיִם אֵל־הַכָּבוֹד הִרְעִים
יהוה עַל־מַֽיִם רַבִּים׃

קוֹל יהוה בַּכֹּֽחַ קוֹל יהוה בֶּהָדָר׃
קוֹל יהוה שֹׁבֵר אֲרָזִים וַיְשַׁבֵּר יהוה אֶת־אַרְזֵי הַלְּבָנוֹן׃
וַיַּרְקִידֵם כְּמוֹ־עֵֽגֶל לְבָנוֹן וְשִׂרְיוֹן כְּמוֹ בֶן־רְאֵמִים׃ ←

Mizmor ledavid.
Havu ladonay beney elim, havu ladonay kavod va'oz.
Havu ladonay kevod shemo, hishtaḥavu ladonay behadrat kodesh.
Kol adonay al hamayim, el hakavod hirim.
Adonay al mayim rabim.
Kol adonay bako'aḥ, kol adonay behadar.
Kol adonay shover arazim, vayshaber adonay et arzey halevanon.
Vayarkidem kemo egel, levanon vesiryon kemo ven re'emim. ↩

The voice of $\frac{\text{YAH}}{\text{THE JUST ONE}}$ hewing flames of fire,

the voice of $\frac{\text{YAH}}{\text{THE ANOINTER}}$ making the desert writhe,
of $\frac{\text{YAH}}{\text{REVIVER}}$ giving the Kadesh desert pangs,

the voice of $\frac{\text{YAH}}{\text{THE MIGHTY ONE}}$ convulsing all the deer,
stripping the forests,
while amid God's palace all declare: "The Glory!"

$\frac{\text{YAH}}{\text{THE REDEEMER}}$ prevailing at the Sea,
$\frac{\text{YAH}}{\text{THE PRESENCE}}$ presiding for the cosmos,

$\frac{\text{YAH}}{\text{THE WANDERER}}$ imparting strength to Israel,
$\frac{\text{YAH}}{\text{GIVER OF WORDS}}$ blessing the people in their peace.

NOTE. The psalm acknowledges the four directions, with Jerusalem as the peaceful center.

מים / waters. Like many storms in Israel, this one starts in the west, over the Mediterranean Sea.

ארזים / cedars, a symbol of something solid and lasting. The storm breaks in the high north, towards Lebanon.

שריון / Sirion—Mt. Hermon, towering on Israel's northern border. Even these mountains quake!

מדבר / desert—the Jordan Valley and the Judean Desert, as the storm moves south-east.

מדבר קדש / wilds of Kadesh south of Jerusalem. L.W.K.

קוֹל יהוה חֹצֵב לַהֲבוֹת אֵשׁ׃

קוֹל יהוה יָחִיל מִדְבָּר   יָחִיל יהוה מִדְבַּר קָדֵשׁ׃
קוֹל יהוה יְחוֹלֵל אַיָּלוֹת   וַיֶּחֱשֹׂף יְעָרוֹת
וּבְהֵיכָלוֹ כֻּלּוֹ אֹמֵר כָּבוֹד׃

יהוה לַמַּבּוּל יָשָׁב   וַיֵּשֶׁב יהוה מֶלֶךְ לְעוֹלָם׃
יהוה עֹז לְעַמּוֹ יִתֵּן   יהוה יְבָרֵךְ אֶת־עַמּוֹ בַשָּׁלוֹם׃

Kol adonay ḥotzev lahavot esh.
Kol adonay yaḥil midbar, yaḥil adonay midbar kadesh.
Kol adonay yeḥolel ayalot, vayeḥesof ye'arot.
Uvheyḥalo kulo omer kavod.
Adonay lamabul yashav, vayeshev adonay meleh le'olam.
Adonay oz le'amo yiten, adonay yevareḥ et amo vashalom.

LEḤAH DODI / O, COME, MY FRIEND

This translation can be sung to the same melody as the Hebrew.

O, come, my friend, let's greet the bride,
the Sabbath Presence bring inside.

"Keep" and "Remember" in a sole command
the solitary God did us command
"I AM!" is one, the Name is one,
in name, in splendor, and in praise.

O, come, my friend, let's greet the bride,
the Sabbath Presence bring inside. ↩

COMMENTARY. Six psalms, one for each weekday, open the traditional *Kabbalat Shabbat* service. The seventh element, the Shabbat psalm, is introduced by the song *Leḥah Dodi,* "Come, My Friend." As Shabbat eve drew near, the Safed Kabbalists used to walk into the fields at the edge of their mountain village in order to greet the day of rest. There they could survey the beauty of creation apparent in the panorama spread before them: mountain, valley, forest, sky, and sea. Through the preceding psalms they gave voice to their praise of creation, and they honored Shabbat with specially composed hymns sung as they escorted Shabbat to their homes.

Leḥah Dodi—a hymn to honor and escort Shabbat—was composed by Shelomo Halevi Alkabetz, a member of the Safed Kabbalists. The initial letters of the poem's first eight stanzas spell out his name: שלמה הלוי. The opening refrain and closing verse of the poem reflect the customs of R. Ḥanina and R. Yanay. Their images of Shabbat as queen and bride combine to link the formal and intimate aspects of Shabbat, the source of all blessing and ultimate intention of creation.

The hymn draws heavily upon prophecies of Israel's redemption and renewal in the messianic era—likened, in Jewish tradition, to a Shabbat without end. Shabbat stands in relation to the week as the messianic era stands in relation to the flow of world time. It is at once a celebration of the world's beginning and a foretaste of the world to come, a reservoir of past and future held in a single moment. S.S.

לְכָה דוֹדִי

לְכָה דוֹדִי לִקְרַאת כַּלָּה פְּנֵי שַׁבָּת נְקַבְּלָה:

שָׁמוֹר וְזָכוֹר בְּדִבּוּר אֶחָד
הִשְׁמִיעָֽנוּ אֵל הַמְיֻחָד
יהוה אֶחָד וּשְׁמוֹ אֶחָד
לְשֵׁם וּלְתִפְאֶֽרֶת וְלִתְהִלָּה: לכה דודי . . . ←

Leḥah dodi likrat kalah peney shabbat nekabelah.

Shamor vezaḥor bedibur eḥad
Hishmi'a̲nu el hamyuḥad
Adonay eḥad ushmo eḥad
Leshem ultife̲ret velit-hilah. Leḥah dodi . . . ↩

NOTE. Biblical references include Isaiah 52:2, 51:17, 60:1; Judges 5:12; Isaiah 60:1, 54:4; Psalm 42:12; Isaiah 14:32; Jeremiah 30:18, 16; Isaiah 49:19, 62:5, 54:3, and 25:9.

NOTE. The first stanza of *Leḥah Dodi* attempts to reconcile two versions (in the Ten Commandments) of the mitzvah to observe Shabbat. The integrity of both "remember the Sabbath day" (Exodus 20:8) and "keep the Sabbath day" (Deuteronomy 5:12) is maintained when the song proclaims that God—in whom all things unite—uttered both simultaneously (Babylonian Talmud, Shevuot 20b). S.S.

Toward the Sabbath, come, make haste,
for she has every blessing's taste,
ordained at first, and long ago,
the last thing made, the first in mind.

> O, come, my friend, let's greet the bride,
> the Sabbath Presence bring inside.

O, Sovereign's abode, O, holy, regal town,
rise up, emerge, where once cast down,
enough of sitting in the vale of tears,
God pities you, yes you God spares.

> O, come, my friend, let's greet the bride,
> the Sabbath Presence bring inside.

Be stirred, rise up, throw off the dust,
my people, don your clothes of eminence,
by hand of Bethle'mite Jesse's child,
draw near my soul, redeem it, too.

> O, come, my friend, let's greet the bride,
> the Sabbath Presence bring inside.

KAVANAH. The lovesong of *Kabbalat Shabbat* continues from *Yedid Nefesh,* Beloved of My Soul, to the Song of Songs, My Beloved is Mine, to *Leḥah Dodi,* Come My Beloved. Stripped away of the work, worry and stress of the week, all that remains is love—love in myriad verbal garments, in myriad melodies. Our pause on the seventh day allows us to fill our beings with love, ever flowing forth from creation. S.P.W.

לִקְרַאת שַׁבָּת לְכוּ וְנֵלְכָה
כִּי הִיא מְקוֹר הַבְּרָכָה
מֵרֹאשׁ מִקֶּֽדֶם נְסוּכָה
סוֹף מַעֲשֶׂה בְּמַחֲשָׁבָה תְּחִלָּה: לכה דודי . . .

מִקְדַּשׁ מֶֽלֶךְ עִיר מְלוּכָה
קֽוּמִי צְאִי מִתּוֹךְ הַהֲפֵכָה
רַב לָךְ שֶֽׁבֶת בְּעֵֽמֶק הַבָּכָא
וְהוּא יַחֲמֹל עָלַֽיִךְ חֶמְלָה: לכה דודי . . .

הִתְנַעֲרִי מֵעָפָר קֽוּמִי
לִבְשִׁי בִּגְדֵי תִפְאַרְתֵּךְ עַמִּי
עַל־יַד בֶּן יִשַׁי בֵּית הַלַּחְמִי
קָרְבָה אֶל נַפְשִׁי גְּאָלָהּ: לכה דודי . . . ←

Likrat shabbat leḥu venelḥah
Ki hi mekor haberaḥah
Merosh mikedem nesuḥah
Sof ma'aseh bemaḥashavah teḥilah. Leḥah dodi . . .

Mikdash meleḥ ir meluḥah
Kumi tze'i mitoḥ hahafeḥa
Rav laḥ shevet be'emek habaḥa
Vehu yaḥamol alayiḥ ḥemlah. Leḥah dodi . . .

Hitna'ari me'afar kumi
Livshi bigdey tifarteḥ ami
Al yad ben yishay beyt halaḥmi
Korvah el nafshi ge'alah. Leḥah dodi . . . ↩

Arouse yourself, arouse yourself,
your light has come, arise and shine,
awake, awake, pour forth your song,
on you now shines the Glorious One.

O, come, my friend, let's greet the bride,
the Sabbath Presence bring inside.

Don't be abashed, don't be ashamed,
why be downcast, why do you sigh?
In you my people's poor find shade,
a city rebuilt where her ruins lay.

O, come, my friend, let's greet the bride,
the Sabbath Presence bring inside.

Your robbers shall be robbed themselves,
all your devourers will be removed,
your God rejoices at your side,
the joy of a bridegroom with his bride.

O, come, my friend, let's greet the bride,
the Sabbath Presence bring inside.

COMMENTARY. Shabbat is here depicted in a glorious array of symbols that derive from the many terms Kabbalistic tradition has used to describe the *Sheḥinah.* She is the bride, the queen, Jerusalem the holy city too long prisoner in the vale of tears, the people Israel about to be crowned with the glory of God. All of these draw together in the single figure of Shabbat as we welcome her into our hearts. A.G.

KAVANAH. God should be so real to us that, in place of the fear and distrust which overcloud our lives, we should be possessed of such peace, poise, and power as to render us free and joyful and give us a sense of dominion. M.M.K.

הִתְעוֹרְרִי הִתְעוֹרְרִי
כִּי בָא אוֹרֵךְ קֽוּמִי אֽוֹרִי
עֽוּרִי עֽוּרִי שִׁיר דַּבֵּֽרִי
כְּבוֹד יהוה עָלַֽיִךְ נִגְלָה: לכה דודי . . .

לֹא תֵבֹֽשִׁי וְלֹא תִכָּלְמִי
מַה תִּשְׁתּוֹחֲחִי וּמַה תֶּהֱמִי
בָּךְ יֶחֱסוּ עֲנִיֵּי עַמִּי
וְנִבְנְתָה עִיר עַל תִּלָּהּ: לכה דודי . . .

וְהָיוּ לִמְשִׁסָּה שֹׁאסָֽיִךְ
וְרָחֲקוּ כָּל־מְבַלְּעָֽיִךְ
יָשִׂישׂ עָלַֽיִךְ אֱלֹהָֽיִךְ
כִּמְשׂוֹשׂ חָתָן עַל כַּלָּה: לכה דודי . . . ←

Hitoreri hitoreri
Ki va oreḥ kumi ori
Uri uri shir daberi
Kevod adonay alayiḥ niglah. Leḥah dodi . . .

Lo tevoshi velo tikalemi
Mah tishtoḥaḥi umah tehemi
Baḥ yeḥesu aniyey ami
Venivnetah ir al tilah. Leḥah dodi . . .

Vehayu limshisah shosayiḥ
Veraḥaku kol mevale'ayiḥ
Yasis alayiḥ elohayiḥ
Kimsos ḥatan al kalah. Leḥah dodi . . . ←

To right and left you shall burst forth,
revering God, to south and north,
by hand of one from Peretz's line,
we shall rejoice and find delight.

> O, come, my friend, let's greet the bride,
> the Sabbath Presence bring inside.

We rise and face the entrance to welcome the Shabbat bride.

O, come in peace, O divine crown,
with joy, rejoicing, and with mirth,
amid the faithful, loved by God,
come in, O bride, come in, O bride!

> O, come, my friend, let's greet the bride,
> the Sabbath Presence bring inside.

בואי בשלום / *Bo'i veshalom,* the last verse of *Leḥah Dodi,* should be recited outdoors. Where this is not possible, a turn toward the doorway is traditional. At *Bo'i ḥalah* (Come in, O bride), we receive into ourselves the *neshamah yeterah,* an extra measure of soul, that is not present to us during the week. This extra Shabbat soul may be viewed as the greater sensitivity allowed us by the restful and unpressured pace of Shabbat. Indeed, that extra soul may be inside us all the time, and *Leḥah Dodi* may be seen as a love song that coaxes our most sensitive self to come out of hiding, in the assurance that on Shabbat it will not be harmed or threatened. A.G.

יָמִין וּשְׂמֹאל תִּפְרֹֽצִי
וְאֶת יהוה תַּעֲרִֽיצִי
עַל יַד אִישׁ בֶּן פַּרְצִי
וְנִשְׂמְחָה וְנָגִֽילָה׃   לכה דודי . . .

We rise and face the entrance to welcome the Shabbat bride.

בֹּֽאִי בְשָׁלוֹם עֲטֶֽרֶת בַּעְלָהּ
גַּם בְּשִׂמְחָה וּבְצָהֳלָה
תּוֹךְ אֱמוּנֵי עַם סְגֻלָּה
בֹּֽאִי כַלָּה בֹּֽאִי כַלָּה׃   לכה דודי . . .

Yamin usmol tifrotzi
Ve'et adonay ta'aritzi
Al yad ish ben partzi
Venismeḥah venagilah.   Leḥah dodi . . .

Bo'i veshalom ateret ba-lah
Gam besimḥah uvtzoholah
Toḥ emuney am segulah
Bo'i ḥalah bo'i ḥalah.   Leḥah dodi . . .

DERASH. There is a Yiddish saying: בײַ „בואי בשלום" שטײט דער אָרעמאַן אויבן אָן / *Bay "bo'i veshalom" shteyt der oreman oybn on.* "During Shabbos prayers, when the entire congregation turns its back to the altar, the pauper standing at the back is suddenly in the front." When the entire congregation turns to the back, inviting the Shabbos queen to come in peace, it is the poor, the shy, and the stranger in the back rows who are given the honor of welcoming her first. She comes in peace only where Jews act responsibly toward those who received this honor.   E.M.

ז

Psalm 92

שבת

A psalm. A song for the day of Shabbat.

It's good to offer thanks to YAH/THE CELESTIAL
to sing out to your name supreme,

to tell about your kindness in the morning,
and your faithfulness at night,
on ten-stringed lyre and on flute,
with melodies conceived on harp,

for you, YAH/GREAT ONE elate me with your deeds,
I'll sing about the actions of your hands.

How great your deeds have been, YAH/SOURCE OF WONDER·
your thoughts exceedingly profound.

Of this the foolish person cannot know,
of this the shallow cannot understand. ↩

NOTE. Psalms 92 and 93 continue the motifs of wholeness, joy, and rest in Shabbat. Psalm 92 has been associated with Shabbat since biblical times. According to the midrash,* Shabbat itself stood up and recited this psalm at Creation, thus exulting in the role given it as the day of inner joy for all of God's creatures. A.G.

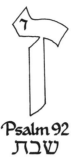

מִזְמוֹר שִׁיר לְיוֹם הַשַּׁבָּת׃

טוֹב לְהֹדוֹת לַיהוה וּלְזַמֵּר לְשִׁמְךָ עֶלְיוֹן׃
לְהַגִּיד בַּבֹּקֶר חַסְדֶּךָ וֶאֱמוּנָתְךָ בַּלֵּילוֹת׃
עֲלֵי־עָשׂוֹר וַעֲלֵי־נָבֶל עֲלֵי הִגָּיוֹן בְּכִנּוֹר׃
כִּי שִׂמַּחְתַּנִי יהוה בְּפָעֳלֶךָ בְּמַעֲשֵׂי יָדֶיךָ אֲרַנֵּן׃
מַה־גָּדְלוּ מַעֲשֶׂיךָ יהוה מְאֹד עָמְקוּ מַחְשְׁבֹתֶיךָ׃
אִישׁ־בַּעַר לֹא יֵדָע וּכְסִיל לֹא־יָבִין אֶת־זֹאת׃←

Mizmor shir leyom hashabbat.

---

*Midrash is a genre of interpretative commentary that derives its name from the root דרש: to seek or search out. The activity of expounding midrash is one of elucidation through creative expansion of words, verses, or whole stories that are ambiguous in the biblical text. These provide fertile ground for imaginative explanation. Midrashic literature dates back to the period of the early Amoraic rabbis, ca. 400 C.E., and is still being created today. M.P.

For though the wicked multiply like weeds,
and evildoers sprout up all around,

it is for their destruction for all time,
but you, YAH/MAJESTY are lifted high eternally,

behold your enemies, YAH/WISE ONE
behold, your enemies are lost,

all evildoers shall be scattered.

You raise my horn like that of the triumphant ox;
I am anointed with fresh oil.
My eye shall gaze in victory on my enemies,
on all who rise against me to do harm;

my ears shall hear of their demise.

The righteous flourish like the palm trees,
like cedars of Lebanon they grow,
implanted in the house of YAH/THE ALL-KNOWING
amid the courtyards of our God they bear fruit.

In their old age, they'll put forth seed,
fleshy and fresh they'll ever be,
to tell the uprightness of YAH/THE MATCHLESS
my Rock, in whom no fault resides.

בִּפְרֹחַ רְשָׁעִים כְּמוֹ־עֵשֶׂב וַיָּצִיצוּ כׇּל־פֹּעֲלֵי אָוֶן
לְהִשָּׁמְדָם עֲדֵי־עַד׃ וְאַתָּה מָרוֹם לְעֹלָם יהוה׃
כִּי הִנֵּה אֹיְבֶיךָ יהוה כִּי־הִנֵּה אֹיְבֶיךָ יֹאבֵדוּ
יִתְפָּרְדוּ כׇּל־פֹּעֲלֵי אָוֶן׃

וַתָּרֶם כִּרְאֵים קַרְנִי בַּלֹּתִי בְּשֶׁמֶן רַעֲנָן׃
וַתַּבֵּט עֵינִי בְּשׁוּרָי בַּקָּמִים עָלַי מְרֵעִים
תִּשְׁמַעְנָה אׇזְנָי׃

צַדִּיק כַּתָּמָר יִפְרָח כְּאֶרֶז בַּלְּבָנוֹן יִשְׂגֶּה׃
שְׁתוּלִים בְּבֵית יהוה בְּחַצְרוֹת אֱלֹהֵינוּ יַפְרִיחוּ׃
עוֹד יְנוּבוּן בְּשֵׂיבָה דְּשֵׁנִים וְרַעֲנַנִּים יִהְיוּ׃
לְהַגִּיד כִּי־יָשָׁר יהוה צוּרִי וְלֹא־עַוְלָתָה בּוֹ׃

Tzadik katamar yifraḥ, ke'erez balvanon yisgeh.
Shetulim beveyt adonay, beḥatzrot eloheynu yafriḥu.
Od yenuvun beseyvah, deshenim vera'ananim yihyu.
Lehagid ki yashar adonay, tzuri velo avlatah bo.

Psalm 93

YAH / THE SUBLIME ONE reigns, clothed in majesty,
YAH / THE LIGHT is clothed, is girded with might.

The world is now established,
it cannot give way.

Your throne was long ago secured,
beyond eternity are you.
The rivers raise, YAH / SOURCE OF LIFE,
the rivers raise a roaring sound,

the floods raise up torrential waves,

but louder than the sound of mighty waters,
more exalted than the breakers of the sea,

raised up on high are you, YAH / INEXPRESSIBLE.

Your precepts have retained their truth,
and holiness befits your house,

YAH / THE GRACIOUS ONE forever.

DERASH. Why does this psalm (93) follow the psalm for Shabbat (92)? In it God watches the seas. The midrash notes that just as earth was created by parting the waters, so was Redemption created by parting the waters. In Creation land was redeemed from the waters. In Redemption human freedom is created. The creation of Shabbat planted the seed of human redemption. The experience of Shabbat nurtures that seed, giving us the strength to quell the floods in our time. D.A.T./S.D.R.

יהוה מָלָךְ גֵּאוּת לָבֵשׁ לָבֵשׁ יהוה עֹז הִתְאַזָּר
אַף־תִּכּוֹן תֵּבֵל בַּל־תִּמּוֹט׃

נָכוֹן כִּסְאֲךָ מֵאָז מֵעוֹלָם אָתָּה׃
נָשְׂאוּ נְהָרוֹת יהוה נָשְׂאוּ נְהָרוֹת קוֹלָם
יִשְׂאוּ נְהָרוֹת דָּכְיָם׃

מִקֹּלוֹת מַ֫יִם רַבִּים אַדִּירִים מִשְׁבְּרֵי־יָם
אַדִּיר בַּמָּרוֹם יהוה׃
עֵדֹתֶ֫יךָ נֶאֶמְנוּ מְאֹד לְבֵיתְךָ נַאֲוָה־קֹ֫דֶשׁ
יהוה לְאֹ֫רֶךְ יָמִים׃

COMMENTARY. Psalm 93 concludes *Kabbalat Shabbat* by retelling the ancient tale of Creation. The waters raised a great shout, showing their power to overwhelm the dry land as it first emerged. So do the forces of chaos and destruction threaten the islands of peace and security we manage to create in our lives. The psalmist assures us, however, that the voice of God is greater than that of even the fiercest storm tides of the ocean. With God's throne firmly established, the peace of Shabbat is now triumphant.

A.G.

ḤATZI KADDISH / SHORT KADDISH

Reader: Let God's name be made great and holy in the world that was created as God willed. May God complete the holy realm in your own lifetime, in your days, and in the days of all the house of Israel, quickly and soon. And say: Amen.

Congregation: May God's great name be blessed, forever and as long as worlds endure.

Reader: May it be blessed, and praised, and glorified, and held in honor, viewed with awe, embellished, and revered; and may the blessed name of holiness be hailed, though it be higher (*On Shabbat Shuvah add:* by far) than all the blessings, songs, praises, and consolations that we utter in this world. And say: Amen.

חֲצִי קַדִּישׁ

יִתְגַּדַּל וְיִתְקַדַּשׁ שְׁמֵהּ רַבָּא בְּעָלְמָא דִּי בְרָא כִרְעוּתֵהּ
וְיַמְלִיךְ מַלְכוּתֵהּ בְּחַיֵּיכוֹן וּבְיוֹמֵיכוֹן וּבְחַיֵּי דְכָל בֵּית יִשְׂרָאֵל
בַּעֲגָלָא וּבִזְמַן קָרִיב וְאִמְרוּ אָמֵן:
יְהֵא שְׁמֵהּ רַבָּא מְבָרַךְ לְעָלַם וּלְעָלְמֵי עָלְמַיָּא:
יִתְבָּרַךְ וְיִשְׁתַּבַּח וְיִתְפָּאַר וְיִתְרוֹמַם וְיִתְנַשֵּׂא וְיִתְהַדַּר וְיִתְעַלֶּה
וְיִתְהַלַּל שְׁמֵהּ דְּקֻדְשָׁא בְּרִיךְ הוּא
לְעֵֽלָּא (*On Shabbat Shuvah add:* לְעֵֽלָּא) מִן כָּל בִּרְכָתָא וְשִׁירָתָא
תֻּשְׁבְּחָתָא וְנֶחֱמָתָא דַּאֲמִירָן בְּעָלְמָא וְאִמְרוּ אָמֵן:

Reader: Yitgadal veyitkadash shemeh raba
be'alma divra ḥiruteh veyamliḥ malḥuteh
beḥayeyḥon uvyomeyḥon uvḥayey deḥol beyt yisra'el
ba'agala uvizman kariv ve'imru amen.

Congregation: Yehey shemeh raba mevaraḥ le'alam ulalmey almaya.

Reader: Yitbaraḥ veyishtabaḥ veyitpa'ar veyitromam
veyitnasey veyit-hadar veyitaleh veyit-halal
shemeh dekudsha beriḥ hu
le'ela (*On Shabbat Shuvah add:* le'ela) min kol birḥata veshirata
tushbeḥata veneḥemata da'amiran be'alma ve'imru amen.

MA'ARIV

THE SHEMA AND ITS BLESSINGS

When a minyan is present, the Bareḥu *is said. The congregation rises and faces the ark. It is customary to bow.*

Reader: Bless $\frac{\text{YAH}}{\text{THE INFINITE}}$ the blessed One!

Congregation: Blessed is $\frac{\text{YAH}}{\text{THE INFINITE}}$ the blessed One, now and forever.

KAVANAH. Public worship aids us by liberating personality from the confining walls of the individual ego. Imprisoned in self, we easily fall prey to morbid brooding. Interference with career, personal disappointment and disillusionment, hurts to vanity, the fear of death—all these tend so to dominate our attention that our minds move in a fixed and narrow system of ideas, which we detest but from which we see no escape. With a whole wide world of boundless opportunities about us, we permit our minds, as it were, to pace up and down within the narrow cell of their ego-prisons. But participation in public worship breaks through the prison of the ego and lets in the light and air of the world. Instead of living but one small and petty life, we now share the multitudinous life of our people. Against the wider horizons that now open to our ken, personal cares do not loom so large. Life becomes infinitely more meaningful and worthwhile when we become aware, through our participation in public worship, of a common life that transcends our individual selves.

M.M.K. (ADAPTED)

מַעֲרִיב

When a minyan is present, the Bareḥu *is said. The congregation rises and faces the ark. It is customary to bow.*

בָּרְכוּ אֶת יהוה הַמְבֹרָךְ:
בָּרוּךְ יהוה הַמְבֹרָךְ לְעוֹלָם וָעֶד:

Bareḥu et adonay hamvoraḥ.
Baruḥ adonay hamvoraḥ le'olam va'ed.

KAVANAH. When we worship in public we know our life is part of a larger life, a wave of an ocean of being—this first-hand experience of that larger life which is God. M.M.K.

COMMENTARY. *Ma'ariv* is the heart of the Friday evening service. As on weekdays, it contains several parts: the Shema and its blessings, the Amidah (silent prayer), and the *Aleynu*. On Shabbat there are several additions: *Veshameru* (Exodus 31:16–17), a brief reprise of the Amidah, and Kiddush. D.A.T.

ASHER BIDVARO / GOD IN NATURE

For additional readings see pages 187–195.

TRADITIONAL VERSION

Blessed are you, YAH / ETERNAL ONE our God, sovereign of all worlds, by whose word the evenings fall. In wisdom you open heaven's gates. With divine discernment you make seasons change, causing the times to come and go, and ordering the stars on their appointed paths through heaven's dome, all according to your will. Creator of the day and night, who rolls back light before the dark, and dark before the light, who makes day pass away and brings on night, dividing between day and night: The Leader of the Throngs of Heaven is your name! Living and enduring God, rule over us, now and always. Blessed are you, YAH / ENDLESS ONE who makes the evenings fall.

DERASH. When we are about to say: "Blessed are you, our God, sovereign of all worlds," and prepare to utter the first word "blessed," we should do so with all our strength, so that we will have no strength left to say, "are you." And this is the meaning of the verse in the Scriptures: "But they that wait for God shall exchange their strength." What we are really saying is: "Source of life, I am giving you all the strength that is within me in that very first word; now will you, in exchange, give me an abundance of new strength, so that I can go on with my prayer."

M.B. (ADAPTED)

אור, חושך, אור / light, dark, light. The words roll into each other just as day rolls into night. They are not separate realms. They mix together. God rules both light and darkness. בין / *beyn:* between. Related to בינה / *binah* and תבונה / *tevunah:* understanding. Wisdom is the ability to distinguish between things, to make sense out of confusion. L.W.K.

אֲשֶׁר בִּדְבָרוֹ

בָּרוּךְ אַתָּה יהוה אֱלֹהֵינוּ מֶלֶךְ הָעוֹלָם אֲשֶׁר בִּדְבָרוֹ מַעֲרִיב עֲרָבִים בְּחָכְמָה פּוֹתֵחַ שְׁעָרִים וּבִתְבוּנָה מְשַׁנֶּה עִתִּים וּמַחֲלִיף אֶת הַזְּמַנִּים וּמְסַדֵּר אֶת־הַכּוֹכָבִים בְּמִשְׁמְרוֹתֵיהֶם בָּרָקִיעַ כִּרְצוֹנוֹ: בּוֹרֵא יוֹם וָלָיְלָה גּוֹלֵל אוֹר מִפְּנֵי חֹשֶׁךְ וְחֹשֶׁךְ מִפְּנֵי אוֹר: וּמַעֲבִיר יוֹם וּמֵבִיא לָיְלָה וּמַבְדִּיל בֵּין יוֹם וּבֵין לָיְלָה יהוה צְבָאוֹת שְׁמוֹ: אֵל חַי וְקַיָּם תָּמִיד יִמְלֹךְ עָלֵינוּ לְעוֹלָם וָעֶד: בָּרוּךְ אַתָּה יהוה הַמַּעֲרִיב עֲרָבִים:

אשר בדברו מעריב ערבים / By whose word the evenings fall. The word plays a central role in the Jewish imagination. Our liturgy fantasizes that God brings on evening each night by saying "Evening!" Thus we repeat each day the original act of Creation that took place by means of the divine word. It is only because we affirm a God who so values language that we feel ourselves able to use words in prayer. Our word, perhaps like God's, gives expression to a depth that goes beyond language, but that can be shared only through the symbolic power of speech. A.G.

COMMENTARY. The two *berahot* which precede the Shema set the stage for its evening recitation. The first *berahah* praises God for the wonders of creation that are visible at twilight: the shifting pattern of the stars, the rhythm of the seasons, the regular passage from day to night. All of these are a nightly reminder of the unchanging plan of creation.

The second *berahah* praises God, whose instruction is a special token of love for Israel. Israel responds by meditating upon God's teaching "day and night," "when we lie down and when we rise." This phrasing recalls the preceding *berahah,* adding Israel's study of Torah to the natural order: The sun sets, the stars shine, and Israel studies—as regularly as day and night. The phrase "when we lie down and when we rise" anticipates the Shema, which follows. This interplay between the *berahot* and the Shema suggests that the Shema is Israel's morning and evening Torah study. At the same time, it is Israel's declaration of the oneness of the power that makes for the natural order and for learning, for creation and human creativity. S.S.

INTERPRETIVE VERSION: ASHER BIDVARO

Praised are you, God, ruler of the universe, who has ordained the rhythm of life. The day with its light calls to activity and exertion. But when the day wanes, when, with the setting of the sun, colors fade, we cease from our labors and welcome the tranquility of the night. The subdued light of the moon and stars, the darkness and the stillness about us invite rest and repose. Trustfully we yield to the quiet of sleep, for we know that, while we are unaware of what goes on within and around us, our powers of body and mind are renewed. Therefore, at this evening hour, we seek composure of spirit. We give thanks for the day and its tasks and for the night and its rest. Praised are you, God, who brings on the evening.

1945 Reconstructionist Prayer Book (adapted)

INTERPRETIVE VERSION: AHAVAT OLAM

We are loved by an unending love.
We are embraced by arms that find us
even when we are hidden from ourselves.

We are touched by fingers that soothe us
even when we are too proud for soothing.
We are counseled by voices that guide us
even when we are too embittered to hear.
We are loved by an unending love.

We are supported by hands that uplift us
even in the midst of a fall.
We are urged on by eyes that meet us
even when we are too weak for meeting.
We are loved by an unending love.

Embraced, touched, soothed, and counseled . . .
ours are the arms, the fingers, the voices;
ours are the hands, the eyes, the smiles;
We are loved by an unending love.

Blessed are you $\frac{\text{YAH}}{\text{MATCHLESS ONE}}$ who loves your people Israel.

Rami M. Shapiro (adapted)

AHAVAT OLAM / GOD'S LOVE IN TORAH

For additional readings see pages 200–201, 203–205.

TRADITIONAL VERSION

With everlasting love, you love the house of Israel. Torah and mitzvot, laws and justice you have taught us. And so, YAH / THE BOUNTIFUL our God, when we lie down and when we rise, we reflect upon your laws; we take pleasure in your Torah's words and your mitzvot, now and always. Truly, they are our life, our length of days. On them we meditate by day and night. Your love will never depart from us as long as worlds endure. Blessed are you, YAH / MATCHLESS ONE who loves your people Israel.

KAVANAH. The שמע/Shema is wrapped in אהבה/*ahavah,* love. The blessing preceding the Shema concludes, "who loves your people Israel." This prayer begins "ואהבת/*ve'ahavta,* And you must love יהוה!" First you are loved, then you respond with love. Love is central to Jewish life. Love means commitment and limitations—Torah and mitzvot. That is so both in our relationships with each other and in our relationship with God.

L.W.K.

DERASH. The term *Sheḥinah* implies that God is not aloof from human life with all its defeats and triumphs. God is in the very midst of life. The rabbis say that when people suffer for their sins, the *Sheḥinah* cries out. The *Sheḥinah* thus moves from Israel to all humanity. M.M.K. (ADAPTED)

אַהֲבַת עוֹלָם

אַהֲבַת עוֹלָם בֵּית יִשְׂרָאֵל עַמְּךָ אָהָבְתָּ: תּוֹרָה וּמִצְוֹת חֻקִּים
וּמִשְׁפָּטִים אוֹתָנוּ לִמַּדְתָּ: עַל כֵּן יהוה אֱלֹהֵינוּ בְּשָׁכְבֵנוּ
וּבְקוּמֵנוּ נָשִׂיחַ בְּחֻקֶּיךָ וְנִשְׂמַח בְּדִבְרֵי תוֹרָתֶךָ וּבְמִצְוֹתֶיךָ לְעוֹלָם
וָעֶד כִּי הֵם חַיֵּינוּ וְאֹרֶךְ יָמֵינוּ וּבָהֶם נֶהְגֶּה יוֹמָם וָלָיְלָה:
וְאַהֲבָתְךָ לֹא תָסוּר מִמֶּנּוּ לְעוֹלָמִים: בָּרוּךְ אַתָּה יהוה אוֹהֵב עַמּוֹ
יִשְׂרָאֵל:

Ahavat olam beyt yisra'el ameḥa ahavta
torah umitzvot ḥukim umishpatim otanu limadeta.
Al ken adonay eloheynu beshoḥvenu uvkumenu nasi'aḥ beḥukeḥa
venismaḥ bedivrey torateḥa uvmitzvoteḥa le'olam va'ed
ki hem ḥayeynu ve'oreḥ yameynu
uvahem nehgeh yomam valaylah.
Ve'ahavateḥa lo tasur mimenu le'olamim.
Baruḥ atah adonay ohev amo yisra'el.

ואהבתך לא תסור. Our text follows the Sephardic version, in the declarative mode ("Your love will never depart from us.") rather than the imperative ("Never remove your love from us!"). Divine love is unconditional. It is available to every one of us when we fashion our lives into channels to receive and share it. The Jewish people together experiences that eternal love as reflected in our love for the study of Torah—a wisdom lovingly received, shared, and passed on enriched by each generation. A.G.

שמע ישראל יהוה אלהינו יהוה אחד

SHEMA

Listen, Israel: YAH/יהוה our God, YAH/יהוה is One!
Blessed be the glory of the Sovereign Name forever.

And you must love YAH/THE ONE your God, with your whole heart, with every breath, with all you have. Take these words that I command you now to heart. Teach them intently to your children; speak them when sitting in your house and walking on the road, when lying down and getting up. Bind them as a sign upon your hand, and keep them visible before your eyes. Write them on the doorposts of your house and on your gates.

שמע . . . ובשעריך / Listen . . . gates (Deuteronomy 6:4–9).

DERASH. The Shema is called *kabbalat ol malḥut shamayim.* We "receive upon ourselves the yoke of the sovereignty of Heaven." To proclaim God as ours and as one is to acknowledge fealty to the divine will—and the Shema is a time to listen. We listen in order to discover God's will.

D.A.T.

ואהבת את יהוה. Love יהוה your God. Abbaye said, "Let the love of God be spread through your activities. If a person studies and helps others to do so, if one's business dealings are decent and trustworthy—what do people say? 'Happy is the one who studied Torah, and the one who teaches Torah! Have you seen the one who studied Torah? How beautiful! What a fine person!' Thus, the Torah says, 'You are my servant Israel; I will be glorified by you'" (Isaiah 49:3). TALMUD YOMA 86A

שְׁמַע יִשְׂרָאֵל יהוה אֱלֹהֵינוּ יהוה | אֶחָד׃

בָּרוּךְ שֵׁם כְּבוֹד מַלְכוּתוֹ לְעוֹלָם וָעֶד׃

וְאָהַבְתָּ אֵת יהוה אֱלֹהֶיךָ בְּכָל־לְבָבְךָ וּבְכָל־נַפְשְׁךָ וּבְכָל־מְאֹדֶךָ׃
וְהָיוּ הַדְּבָרִים הָאֵלֶּה אֲשֶׁר אָנֹכִי מְצַוְּךָ הַיּוֹם עַל־לְבָבֶךָ׃
וְשִׁנַּנְתָּם לְבָנֶיךָ וְדִבַּרְתָּ בָּם בְּשִׁבְתְּךָ בְּבֵיתֶךָ וּבְלֶכְתְּךָ בַדֶּרֶךְ
וּבְשָׁכְבְּךָ וּבְקוּמֶךָ׃ וּקְשַׁרְתָּם לְאוֹת עַל־יָדֶךָ וְהָיוּ לְטֹטָפֹת בֵּין
עֵינֶיךָ׃ וּכְתַבְתָּם עַל־מְזֻזוֹת בֵּיתֶךָ וּבִשְׁעָרֶיךָ׃ ←

Shema yisra'el adonay eloheynu adonay eḥad.
Baruḥ shem kevod malḥuto le'olam va'ed.

Ve'ahavta et adonay eloheḥa
beḥol levaveḥa uvḥol nafsheḥa uvḥol me'odeḥa.
Vehayu hadevarim ha'eleh asher anoḥi metzaveḥa hayom al levaveḥa.
Veshinantam levaneḥa vedibarta bam
beshivteḥa beveyteḥa uvleḥteḥa vadereḥ uvshoḥbeḥa uvkumeḥa.
Ukshartam le'ot al yadeḥa vehayu letotafot beyn eyneḥa.
Uḥtavtam al mezuzot beyteḥa uvishareḥa. ↩

לבבך / *levaveḥa* / your heart. The לב / *lev* / heart, was seen as the source of emotions and intellect. Feelings and reason are complementary partners, not conflicting parts, of the human psyche. The double ב of לבב teaches that a love of God must contain all dualities (e.g., the good and bad in you). L.W.K.

טטפת בין עיניך. *Totafot* might have been pendants or forehead markings. The Torah text sees *totafot* as reminders of the divine will. The English translation captures this figurative meaning of a visible reminder of the mitzvot. D.A.T.

For the second paragraph of the Shema, read either the traditional version below or the contemporary biblical selection beginning on page 76, then continue with the third paragraph, page 80.

TRADITIONAL BIBLICAL SELECTION

If you truly listen to my bidding, as I bid you now—loving YAH / THE FOUNT OF LIFE your God, and serving God with all your heart, with every breath—then I will give you rain upon your land in its appointed time, the early rain and later rain, so you may gather in your corn, your wine and oil. And I will give you grass upon your field to feed your animals, and you will eat and be content. Beware, therefore, lest your heart be led astray, and you go off and serve other gods, and you submit to them, so that YAH / THE MIGHTY ONE's anger should burn against you, and seal up the heavens so no rain would fall, so that the ground would not give forth her produce, and you be forced to leave the good land I am giving you. ↩

DERASH. The traditional second paragraph of the Shema (Deuteronomy 11:13–21) offers an account of the natural process by which the blessings of God themselves lead to pride, self-satisfaction, and ingratitude on the part of those who receive them. Ironically, the more we are blessed, so it seems, the less grateful and aware of blessing we become. It is when we are most sated, Scripture warns us, that we should be most careful. Fullness can lead to ingratitude, and ingratitude to idolatry—primarily in the form of worship of our own accomplishments. Then, indeed, "the heavens might close up and no rain fall." For, once we begin to worship our achievements, we will never find satisfaction. A.G.

DERASH. This warning against idolatry has ecological significance. If we continue to pollute the environment—and thus display contempt for the integrity of God's creation—pure rain will cease to fall, and the ground will cease to give forth its produce. M.L.

For the second paragraph of the Shema, read either the traditional version below or the contemporary biblical selection beginning on page 77, then continue with the third paragraph, page 81.

TRADITIONAL BIBLICAL SELECTION

וְהָיָה אִם־שָׁמֹעַ תִּשְׁמְעוּ אֶל־מִצְוֺתַי אֲשֶׁר אָנֹכִי מְצַוֶּה
אֶתְכֶם הַיּוֹם לְאַהֲבָה אֶת־יהוה אֱלֹהֵיכֶם וּלְעָבְדוֹ בְּכָל־לְבַבְכֶם
וּבְכָל־נַפְשְׁכֶם: וְנָתַתִּי מְטַר־אַרְצְכֶם בְּעִתּוֹ יוֹרֶה וּמַלְקוֹשׁ
וְאָסַפְתָּ דְגָנֶךָ וְתִירֹשְׁךָ וְיִצְהָרֶךָ: וְנָתַתִּי עֵשֶׂב בְּשָׂדְךָ לִבְהֶמְתֶּךָ
וְאָכַלְתָּ וְשָׂבָעְתָּ: הִשָּׁמְרוּ לָכֶם פֶּן־יִפְתֶּה לְבַבְכֶם וְסַרְתֶּם
וַעֲבַדְתֶּם אֱלֹהִים אֲחֵרִים וְהִשְׁתַּחֲוִיתֶם לָהֶם: וְחָרָה אַף־יהוה
בָּכֶם וְעָצַר אֶת־הַשָּׁמַיִם וְלֹא־יִהְיֶה מָטָר וְהָאֲדָמָה לֹא תִתֵּן אֶת־
יְבוּלָהּ וַאֲבַדְתֶּם מְהֵרָה מֵעַל הָאָרֶץ הַטֹּבָה אֲשֶׁר יהוה נֹתֵן לָכֶם: ←

COMMENTARY. The statement of God's oneness unifies not only the context of Shema but the text as well—three scriptural paragraphs specified in the Mishnah (a second century codification of Jewish law). The powerful declaration of God's unity fuses the responsibility to love God and to study God's teachings (first paragraph) with the lesson that their fulfillment confirms God's presence (second and third paragraphs). Hence, the unity of God as idea and presence. S.S.

In the handwritten scroll of the Torah
The word "Shema" of "*Shema Yisra'el*"
Ends with an oversized *ayin,*
And the word "*Eḥad*"
Ends with an oversized *dalet.*
Taken together
These two letters
Spell "*Ed,*" meaning "witness."
    Whenever we recite the Shema
    We bear witness
    To our awareness
    Of God's presence. H.M.

So place these words upon your heart, into your lifebreath. Bind them as a sign upon your hand, and let them rest before your eyes. Teach them to your children, speaking of them when you sit at home and when you walk upon the road, when you lie down and when you rise—so that your days and your children's days be many on the land that YAH / THE CARING ONE promised to give your ancestors for as long as heaven rests above the earth.

Continue with page 80.

CONTEMPORARY BIBLICAL SELECTION

It came to pass, and will again,
that if you truly listen
to the voice of YAH / THE INCOMPARABLE your God,
being sure to do whatever has been asked of you today,
YAH / THE ULTIMATE your God, will make of you a model
for all nations of the earth,
and there will come upon you all these blessings,
as you listen to the call of YAH / THE MANY-NAMED your God:
Blessed be you in the city,
and blessed be you in the field.
Blessed be the fruit of your womb,
the fruit of your land, the fruit of your cattle,
the calving of your oxen, the lambing of your sheep.
Blessed be your basket and your kneading-trough.
Blessed be you when you come home,
and blessed be you when you go out. ↩

וְשַׂמְתֶּם אֶת־דְּבָרַי אֵלֶּה עַל־לְבַבְכֶם וְעַל־נַפְשְׁכֶם וּקְשַׁרְתֶּם אֹתָם
לְאוֹת עַל־יֶדְכֶם וְהָיוּ לְטוֹטָפֹת בֵּין עֵינֵיכֶם: וְלִמַּדְתֶּם אֹתָם אֶת־
בְּנֵיכֶם לְדַבֵּר בָּם בְּשִׁבְתְּךָ בְּבֵיתֶךָ וּבְלֶכְתְּךָ בַדֶּרֶךְ וּבְשָׁכְבְּךָ
וּבְקוּמֶךָ: וּכְתַבְתָּם עַל־מְזוּזוֹת בֵּיתֶךָ וּבִשְׁעָרֶיךָ: לְמַעַן יִרְבּוּ
יְמֵיכֶם וִימֵי בְנֵיכֶם עַל הָאֲדָמָה אֲשֶׁר נִשְׁבַּע יהוה לַאֲבֹתֵיכֶם
לָתֵת לָהֶם כִּימֵי הַשָּׁמַיִם עַל־הָאָרֶץ:

Continue with ויאמר, *page 81.*

CONTEMPORARY BIBLICAL SELECTION

וְהָיָה אִם־שָׁמוֹעַ תִּשְׁמַע בְּקוֹל יהוה אֱלֹהֶיךָ לִשְׁמֹר לַעֲשׂוֹת אֶת־
כָּל־מִצְוֹתָיו אֲשֶׁר אָנֹכִי מְצַוְּךָ הַיּוֹם וּנְתָנְךָ יהוה אֱלֹהֶיךָ עֶלְיוֹן
עַל כָּל־גּוֹיֵי הָאָרֶץ: וּבָאוּ עָלֶיךָ כָּל־הַבְּרָכוֹת הָאֵלֶּה וְהִשִּׂיגֻךָ
כִּי תִשְׁמַע בְּקוֹל יהוה אֱלֹהֶיךָ: בָּרוּךְ אַתָּה בָּעִיר וּבָרוּךְ אַתָּה
בַּשָּׂדֶה: בָּרוּךְ פְּרִי־בִטְנְךָ וּפְרִי אַדְמָתְךָ וּפְרִי בְהֶמְתֶּךָ שְׁגַר
אֲלָפֶיךָ וְעַשְׁתְּרוֹת צֹאנֶךָ: בָּרוּךְ טַנְאֲךָ וּמִשְׁאַרְתֶּךָ: בָּרוּךְ אַתָּה
בְּבֹאֶךָ וּבָרוּךְ אַתָּה בְּצֵאתֶךָ: ←

COMMENTARY. The traditional wording presents detailed bountiful or devastating consequences of Israel's collective relationship to the mitzvot. This biblical section (Deuteronomy 11:13–21) offers a supernatural theology that many contemporary Jews find difficult. The contemporary biblical selection (Deuteronomy 28:1–6, 30:15–19) begins by encouraging observance in the same language, but it concentrates on the positive ways in which observance of mitzvot focuses our attention on God's presence as perceived through productivity and the pursuit of abundant life. S.S.

See, I have placed in front of you today
both life and good, and death and ill,
commanding you today: love $\frac{\text{YAH}}{\text{THE SOURCE}}$ your God,
walking in ways I have ordained,
keeping the commandments, laws, and judgments,
so that you survive and multiply,
and $\frac{\text{YAH}}{\text{THE BENEFICENT}}$ your God, will bless you
on the land you are about to enter and inherit.
But if your heart should turn away,
and you not heed, and go astray,
and you submit to other gods and serve them,
I declare to you today that you shall be
destroyed completely; you shall not live out
a great expanse of days upon the land
that you now cross the Jordan to possess.
I call as witnesses concerning you
both heaven and earth, both life and death,
that I have placed in front of you
a blessing and a curse.
Choose life, that you may live,
you and your seed! ↩

רְאֵה נָתַתִּי לְפָנֶיךָ הַיּוֹם אֶת־הַחַיִּים וְאֶת־הַטּוֹב וְאֶת־הַמָּוֶת וְאֶת־
הָרָע׃ אֲשֶׁר אָנֹכִי מְצַוְּךָ הַיּוֹם לְאַהֲבָה אֶת־יהוה אֱלֹהֶיךָ לָלֶכֶת
בִּדְרָכָיו וְלִשְׁמֹר מִצְוֹתָיו וְחֻקֹּתָיו וּמִשְׁפָּטָיו וְחָיִיתָ וְרָבִיתָ וּבֵרַכְךָ
יהוה אֱלֹהֶיךָ בָּאָרֶץ אֲשֶׁר־אַתָּה בָא־שָׁמָּה לְרִשְׁתָּהּ׃ וְאִם־יִפְנֶה
לְבָבְךָ וְלֹא תִשְׁמָע וְנִדַּחְתָּ וְהִשְׁתַּחֲוִיתָ לֵאלֹהִים אֲחֵרִים
וַעֲבַדְתָּם׃ הִגַּדְתִּי לָכֶם הַיּוֹם כִּי אָבֹד תֹּאבֵדוּן לֹא־תַאֲרִיכֻן יָמִים
עַל־הָאֲדָמָה אֲשֶׁר אַתָּה עֹבֵר אֶת־הַיַּרְדֵּן לָבוֹא שָׁמָּה לְרִשְׁתָּהּ׃
הַעִדֹתִי בָכֶם הַיּוֹם אֶת־הַשָּׁמַיִם וְאֶת־הָאָרֶץ הַחַיִּים וְהַמָּוֶת נָתַתִּי
לְפָנֶיךָ הַבְּרָכָה וְהַקְּלָלָה וּבָחַרְתָּ בַּחַיִּים לְמַעַן תִּחְיֶה אַתָּה וְזַרְעֶךָ׃ ←

KAVANAH. The doctrine of the unity of God calls for the integration of all life's purposes into a consistent pattern of thought and conduct. M.M.K.

DERASH. God is the assumption that there is enough in the world to meet our needs but not to meet our greed for power and pleasure.
M.M.K. (ADAPTED)

YAH / THE VOICE told Moses: Speak to the Israelites—tell them to make themselves *tzitzit* upon the corners of their clothes, throughout their generations. Have them place upon the corner *tzitzit* a twine of royal blue. This is your *tzitzit*. Look at it and remember all the things that I, YAH / THE TRUTH have asked of you. And do them, so you won't go off after the lusts of your heart or after what catches your eye, so that you remember to do all my mitzvot and be holy for your God. I am YAH / THE FAITHFUL ONE your God, who brought you out of Mitzrayim, to be for you a God. I am YAH / THE OMNIPRESENT ONE your God.

ויאמר יהוה . . . אלהיכם / YAH / THE VOICE . . . God (Numbers 15:37–41).

COMMENTARY. In the ancient Near East, free people wore fringes, or *tzitzit,* on the hems of their everyday clothes. Since only free people wore *tzitzit,* they were a form of identification. Business transactions were sealed by kissing the *tzitzit.*

The mitzvah of *tzitzit* is based on that ancient sign of freedom. The fringes remind us that we voluntarily follow the way of God, who freed us from Egyptian slavery. It is, literally, a string tied around our finger.

Today, many Jews who recite the Shema gather the four corners of their *tallitot* (prayer shawls), hold the *tzitzit,* and kiss them at each mention of the word **ציצית** / *tzitzit.* This custom shows that we take these words seriously, like a legal contract. L.W.K.

מצרים / Mitzrayim was the escaping Hebrews', not the Egyptians', name for the land of Egypt: perhaps a slave-term, and probably not of Semitic origin, it has associations with the root **צרר**, to be in distress, constricted, in anguish, or in dire straits. This word powerfully evokes the choking oppression of slavery. As the psalmist wrote: **מן המצר קראתי יה** / From the depths I called to Yah. M.P.

וַיֹּאמֶר יהוה אֶל־מֹשֶׁה לֵּאמֹר: דַּבֵּר אֶל־בְּנֵי יִשְׂרָאֵל וְאָמַרְתָּ
אֲלֵהֶם וְעָשׂוּ לָהֶם צִיצִת עַל־כַּנְפֵי בִגְדֵיהֶם לְדֹרֹתָם וְנָתְנוּ עַל־
צִיצִת הַכָּנָף פְּתִיל תְּכֵלֶת: וְהָיָה לָכֶם לְצִיצִת וּרְאִיתֶם אֹתוֹ
וּזְכַרְתֶּם אֶת־כָּל־מִצְוֺת יהוה וַעֲשִׂיתֶם אֹתָם וְלֹא תָתוּרוּ אַחֲרֵי
לְבַבְכֶם וְאַחֲרֵי עֵינֵיכֶם אֲשֶׁר־אַתֶּם זֹנִים אַחֲרֵיהֶם: לְמַעַן תִּזְכְּרוּ
וַעֲשִׂיתֶם אֶת־כָּל־מִצְוֺתָי וִהְיִיתֶם קְדֹשִׁים לֵאלֹהֵיכֶם: אֲנִי יהוה
אֱלֹהֵיכֶם אֲשֶׁר הוֹצֵאתִי אֶתְכֶם מֵאֶרֶץ מִצְרַיִם לִהְיוֹת לָכֶם
לֵאלֹהִים אֲנִי יהוה אֱלֹהֵיכֶם: יהוה אֱלֹהֵיכֶם אֱמֶת:

כל מצות יהוה / all of God's mitzvot. According to rabbinic tradition, there are 613 mitzvot in the Torah. כל, all, as many as possible. A combination of gematria (Jewish numerology) and ritual macrame "proves" that ציצית / *tzitzit* equals all 613 mitzvot combined: צ = 90, י = 10, צ = 90, י = 10, ת = 400; all together = 600. Each *tzitzit* has 8 strands (per corner) and 5 knots; 8 + 5 = 13; 13 + 600 = 613. L.W.K.

אחרי עיניכם / after what catches your eye, that is, the physical and material temptations you see. The Baal Shem Tov had a method for dealing with distractions, especially sexual ones. If you can't get that person out of your thoughts, remember that beauty is a reflection of God's image. Redirect that energy towards God. L.W.K.

תכלת is Sidon blue, which is obtained from a shellfish. Sidon or royal blue is associated with majesty—even today the British queen wears a blue sash. The Jews were so oppressed at the time of Bar Koḥbah that indigo, a vegetable dye, replaced Sidon blue on their *tzitzit*. The Romans banned the blue fringe because of its symbolism. During the nineteenth century the Radnizer *ḥasidim* reintroduced its use. Now other Jews have also begun to use it. The long *teḥelet* thread intertwined with short white ones is a complex and powerful image that hints at the interplay between majesty and subject within our own hearts. E.M.

EMET VE'EMUNAH / REDEMPTION

The traditional Ge'ulah is on this page; an interpretive version begins on page 84.
For additional readings see pages 196–200, 205.

Our faith and truth rest on all this, which is binding upon us:

That YAH / THE UTMOST alone is our divinity
and that no divinity exists but One;
that we are Israel, community of God;
that it is God who saves us from the hand
of governments, the very palm of tyrants;
who puts our souls amid the living,
and who keeps our feet from giving way;
who breaks apart the schemes of those who hate us,
confounds the thoughts of any bearing us ill-will;
that it is God who made miracles for us in Egypt,
signs and wonders in Ham's children's land.
From one generation to the next, God is our guarantor,
and even on a day that turned to night,
God stayed with us when death's deep shadow fell.
And even in our age of orphans and survivors,
God's loving acts have not abandoned us,
and God has brought together our scattered kin
from the distant corners of the earth.

As then, so now,
God brings the people Israel forth
from every place of menace, to a lasting freedom,
God is the one who brought the Israelites
through a divided Sea of Reeds.
There, they beheld divine might;
they praised and thanked the Name,
and willingly accepted for themselves
God's rule.

Moses and all the Israelites
broke out in song, abundant in their joy,
and, all as one, they said: *(Continue on page 86.)*

אֱמֶת וֶאֱמוּנָה

אֱמֶת וֶאֱמוּנָה כָּל זֹאת וְקַיָּם עָלֵינוּ
כִּי הוּא יהוה אֱלֹהֵינוּ וְאֵין זוּלָתוֹ
וַאֲנַחְנוּ יִשְׂרָאֵל עַמּוֹ:
הַפּוֹדֵנוּ מִיַּד מְלָכִים
הַגּוֹאֲלֵנוּ מִכַּף עָרִיצִים
הָעוֹשֶׂה גְדוֹלוֹת אֵין חֵקֶר
וְנִפְלָאוֹת אֵין מִסְפָּר:
הַשָּׂם נַפְשֵׁנוּ בַּחַיִּים
וְלֹא נָתַן לַמּוֹט רַגְלֵנוּ:
הַמֵּפֵר עֲצַת אוֹיְבֵינוּ
וְהַמְקַלְקֵל מַחְשְׁבוֹת שׂוֹנְאֵינוּ:
הָעוֹשֶׂה לָּנוּ נִסִּים בְּמִצְרַיִם
אוֹתוֹת וּמוֹפְתִים בְּאַדְמַת בְּנֵי חָם:
מִדּוֹר לְדוֹר הוּא גּוֹאֲלֵנוּ:
וּבַיּוֹם שֶׁהָפַךְ לְלַיְלָה
עִמָּנוּ הָיָה בְּגֵיא צַלְמָוֶת:

(Continue on page 85.)

אמת ואמונה. The blessing immediately following the Shema deals with the theme of divine redemption. The present text, a rewritten version, includes reference to the Holocaust, from which there was no redemption, and the return to Zion, a fulfillment of Israel's ancient dream. The same divine spirit that gave Israel the courage to seek freedom from Egypt in ancient times inspired those who fought for Israel's freedom in our own day. At the same time, this version omits those portions of the text that glory in the enemy's fall or see in God a force for vengeance. All humans are God's beloved children, as were the Egyptians who drowned at the sea.

A.G.

INTERPRETIVE VERSION

We acknowledge as true and trustworthy that there is but one universal God, and that to God's service Israel stands eternally committed.

We recognize in God the power that has enabled us to triumph over defeat, persecution and oppression.

It was God who redeemed us from Egyptian bondage, and delivered us from the despotism of the pharaohs.

For God wills that we be free to use our powers in holy service, and be not bound to the arbitrary rule of any mortal.

Whenever human rulers usurp divine authority, and exploit the people, those tyrants' hearts are hardened, their own arrogance writes their doom.

Therefore we will never be discouraged nor dismayed when unrighteous powers rise up to destroy us.

Though enemy hosts pursue us, we shall remember how our ancestors were saved at the Sea of Reeds.

We therefore repeat the words of triumph with which they gave thanks for their deliverance:

1945 Reconstructionist Prayer Book (adapted)

(Congregation sings מי כמכה*,* *page 87)*

COMMENTARY. Two beautiful *beraḥot* complete the liturgical framework of the Shema in the evening service. The first of these is called *Ge'ulah*—"Redemption." Recalling the Exodus from Egypt, it thematically echoes the third paragraph of the Shema. Moreover, it identifies the sovereign God, named in the Shema's credo, as the power that freed Israel from slavery. Its vivid, here-and-now recollection of the escape from Egyptian bondage invites and challenges Israel to claim the redemption as a personal experience in each generation and to hear echoes of that ancient triumph over tyranny in each modern-day struggle for freedom, in every attempt to move toward the messianic future. S.S.

גַּם בְּדוֹר יְתוֹמִים
לֹא עֲזָבוּנוּ חֲסָדָיו
וַיְקַבֵּץ נִדָּחֵינוּ מִקְּצוֹת תֵּבֵל:
כְּאָז גַּם עַתָּה
מוֹצִיא אֶת עַמּוֹ יִשְׂרָאֵל
מִכַּף כָּל אוֹיְבָיו
לְחֵרוּת עוֹלָם:
הַמַּעֲבִיר בָּנָיו בֵּין גִּזְרֵי יַם סוּף
שָׁם רָאוּ אֶת גְּבוּרָתוֹ
שִׁבְּחוּ וְהוֹדוּ לִשְׁמוֹ
וּמַלְכוּתוֹ בְּרָצוֹן קִבְּלוּ עֲלֵיהֶם:

מֹשֶׁה וּבְנֵי יִשְׂרָאֵל לְךָ עָנוּ שִׁירָה בְּשִׂמְחָה רַבָּה וְאָמְרוּ כֻלָּם:

Mosheh uvney yisra'el leḥa anu shirah besimḥah rabah ve'ameru ḥulam.

DERASH. Rabbi Judah said: [At the sea] each tribe said to the other, "You go into the sea first!" As they stood there bickering, Naḥshon ben Aminadav jumped into the water. Meanwhile Moses was praying. God said to him, "My friend is drowning—and you pray!" "What can I do?" Moses asked. [God responded as it says in the text,] "Speak to the people of Israel and tell them to go! Raise your staff. . . ." TALMUD SOTAH 37A

NOTE. Biblical references include Job 9:10, Psalm 66:9.

"Who among the mighty can compare
to you, YAH / GREAT ONE?
Who can compare to you,
adorned in holiness,
awesome in praises,
acting wondrously!"

Your children saw you in your majesty,
splitting the sea in front of Moses.
"This is my God!" they cried, and said:

"YAH / THE HOLY ONE will reign forever!"

And it was said:

"Yes, YAH / THE REDEEMER has rescued Jacob,
saved him
from a power
stronger than his own!"

Blessed are you, YAH / GUARDIAN Israel's redeeming power!

When our ancestors
beheld these truths
they proclaimed:
Among all the gods
we can name,
who can compare to the
One Beyond Naming?
Among all the quantities
we can label, number,
mark and measure,
which compares to the
Mystery
at the Heart of Reality?

R.M.S.

מִי־כָמֹֽכָה בָּאֵלִים יהוה מִי כָּמֹֽכָה נֶאְדָּר בַּקֹּֽדֶשׁ
נוֹרָא תְהִלֹּת עֹֽשֵׂה פֶֽלֶא׃
מַלְכוּתְךָ רָאוּ בָנֶֽיךָ בּוֹקֵֽעַ יָם לִפְנֵי מֹשֶׁה זֶה אֵלִי עָנוּ וְאָמְרוּ׃
יהוה יִמְלֹךְ לְעֹלָם וָעֶד׃
וְנֶאֱמַר׃ כִּי פָדָה יהוה אֶת־יַעֲקֹב וּגְאָלוֹ מִיַּד חָזָק מִמֶּֽנּוּ׃ בָּרוּךְ
אַתָּה יהוה גָּאַל יִשְׂרָאֵל׃

Mi ḥamoḥah ba'elim adonay.
Mi kamoḥah nedar bakodesh
nora tehilot osey feleh.
Malḥuteḥa ra'u vaneḥa boke'a yam lifney mosheh.
Zeh eli anu ve'ameru.
Adonay yimloḥ le'olam va'ed.
Vene'emar ki fadah adonay et ya'akov ugalo miyad ḥazak mimenu.
Baruḥ atah adonay ga'al yisra'el.

בוקע ים לפני משה. This siddur reinstates reference to the splitting of the sea as a sign of God's redeeming power. The earlier Reconstructionist prayerbook omitted that reference because of its emphasis on supernatural intervention. As myth, however, the ancient tale of wonder underscores the sense of daily miracle in our lives. Even those of us who cannot affirm a God who intervenes in the natural process, and thus cannot accept the literal meaning of the tale, can appreciate its human message. According to the midrash, the sea did not split until one Israelite, Naḥshon ben Aminadav, had the courage to walk upright into the water. Perhaps it was the divine spirit in Naḥshon, rather than the magic of Moses's wand, that caused the sea to split. A.G.

NOTE. Biblical references include Exodus 15:11, 18 and Jeremiah 31:11.

ברוך אתה יהוה הפורש סכת שלום

who spreads your harmonious canopy
and over Jerusalem.

HASHKIVENU / DIVINE HELP

For additional readings see pages 196, 200–203, 211.

Help us lie down, YAH / DEAR ONE our God, in peace, and let us rise again, sovereign, to life. Spread over us your shelter of peace. Decree for us a worthy daily lot—for you are our protector and our help. Truly, a sovereign, freely giving, caring God are you. Guard our going forth each day for life and peace, now and always. Spread over us the shelter of your peace.

עלינו ועל-כל-עמו ישראל ועל-ירושלים

Blessed are you, Yah/the Compassionate,
over all your people Israel

הַשְׁכִּיבֵנוּ

הַשְׁכִּיבֵנוּ יהוה אֱלֹהֵינוּ לְשָׁלוֹם וְהַעֲמִידֵנוּ מַלְכֵּנוּ לְחַיִּים וּפְרוֹשׂ עָלֵינוּ סֻכַּת שְׁלוֹמֶךָ: וְתַקְּנֵנוּ בְּעֵצָה טוֹבָה מִלְּפָנֶיךָ וְהוֹשִׁיעֵנוּ לְמַעַן שְׁמֶךָ: וּבְצֵל כְּנָפֶיךָ תַּסְתִּירֵנוּ כִּי אֵל שׁוֹמְרֵנוּ וּמַצִּילֵנוּ אָתָּה כִּי אֵל מֶלֶךְ חַנּוּן וְרַחוּם אָתָּה: וּשְׁמֹר צֵאתֵנוּ וּבוֹאֵנוּ לְחַיִּים וּלְשָׁלוֹם מֵעַתָּה וְעַד עוֹלָם: וּפְרֹשׂ עָלֵינוּ סֻכַּת שְׁלוֹמֶךָ: ←

Blessed are you, $\frac{\text{YAH}}{\text{THE COMPASSIONATE}}$ who spreads your harmonious canopy over all your people Israel and over Jerusalem.

COMMENTARY. *Hashkivenu*—"Help us lie down [in peace]"—is the final prescribed part of the Shema. It recalls the Shema by expressing the hope that we will "lie down . . . in peace" and "rise again . . . to life." An extension of *Emet Ve'emunah, Hashkivenu* joins the vivid recollection of past redemption to a prayer for present protection and future peace. By calling God "guardian" and "protector" but also "redeemer," Israel recognizes new dimensions of the power that makes for freedom. The final acknowledgment of God as the one who "spreads the sukkah of peace over us, over Israel, and over Jerusalem" conjures up the now familiar image of Shabbat as a foretaste of that future time when Israel, its people, and its holy city will dwell in peace. This blessing is unique to the evening service. Perhaps responding to the cold, dark uncertainty of night, we invoke God's dwelling of peace. S.S.

KAVANAH. Enable us, God, to behold meaning in the chaos of life about us and purpose in the chaos of life within us. Deliver us from the sense of futility in our strivings toward the light and the truth. Give us strength to ride safely through the maelstrom of petty cares and anxieties. May we behold things in their proper proportions and see life in its wholeness and its holiness. M.M.K. (ADAPTED)

NOTE. For our ancestors, the future of Jerusalem was not just about the future of the Jewish people. Jerusalem, in the biblical vision, will become the capital of the whole world. Praying for the peace of Jerusalem is the same as praying for the unity of all humanity and peace throughout the world. D.A.T.

בָּרוּךְ אַתָּה יהוה הַפּוֹרֵשׂ סֻכַּת שָׁלוֹם עָלֵינוּ וְעַל כׇּל־עַמּוֹ יִשְׂרָאֵל וְעַל יְרוּשָׁלָיִם:

COMMENTARY. The version presented here follows certain Sephardic versions by deleting the series of petitions for protection. Such petition is considered inappropriate on Shabbat, a day of fulfillment and appreciation for the many blessings we have. Shabbat itself is a sukkah of peace. We pray that real and complete peace be the lot of Israel and Jerusalem, so torn by strife in recent memory. Our tradition sees Jerusalem as the center of the world. Creation began there, according to the rabbis. So may the peace that begins there radiate forth and bless all earth's peoples. The peace of Jerusalem, the "heart of the world," is also the peace of every human heart. A.G.

KAVANAH. As we enter the dark of evening, we face the unknown. Earlier, in *Asher Bidvaro* (the Creation section immediately following *Bareḥu*), we affirmed the power that transforms night into day and day into night. Now we call for protection from the shadows that lengthen around us—shadows of fear and guilt, the uncharted future, the ever pursuing past. We ask that the shadows of God's wings envelop us with love and mercy. The unknown night, like the unknown tomorrow, can only be met with faith in the power of infinite compassion to care for us. S.P.W.

When fears multiply
And danger threatens;
When sickness comes,
When death confronts us—
It is God's blessing of shalom
That sustains us
And upholds us.

Lightening our burden,
Dispelling our worry,
Restoring our strength,
Renewing our hope—
Reviving us.

H.M.

VESHAMERU / OBSERVING SHABBAT

Let Israel's descendants keep Shabbat, making Shabbat throughout all their generations, as an eternal bond. Between me and Israel's descendants shall it be a sign eternally. For in six days YAH / THE VOICE made skies and earth, and on the seventh day God ceased and drew a breath of rest.

(*When Shabbat coincides with a festival, add:*

Moses proclaimed the festivals of YAH / THE ENDURING ONE to the children of Israel.)

NOTE. The placement of *Veshameru* after *Hashkivenu* suggests an aspect of the agreement between God and Israel: God guards Israel, and Israel guards Shabbat, which is a reminder and foretaste of peace in our world.

S.S.

KAVANAH. The recitation of *Veshameru* preceding the Amidah and of *Vayḥulu* following it on Friday evening are acts of witnessing. In keeping Shabbat Israel bears testimony to the fact that ours is a created world. For us this means that divinity fills the universe. Our task is to treat all living things with respect, and so enhance the divine light in them. Only by this way of living is the testimony of Shabbat made real. A.G.

וְשָׁמְרוּ

וְשָׁמְרוּ בְנֵי־יִשְׂרָאֵל אֶת־הַשַּׁבָּת לַעֲשׂוֹת אֶת־הַשַּׁבָּת לְדֹרֹתָם
בְּרִית עוֹלָם: בֵּינִי וּבֵין בְּנֵי יִשְׂרָאֵל אוֹת הִיא לְעוֹלָם כִּי־שֵׁשֶׁת
יָמִים עָשָׂה יהוה אֶת־הַשָּׁמַיִם וְאֶת־הָאָרֶץ וּבַיּוֹם הַשְּׁבִיעִי שָׁבַת
וַיִּנָּפַשׁ:

Veshameru veney yisra'el et hashabbat
la'asot et hashabbat ledorotam berit olam.
Beyni uveyn beney yisra'el ot hi le'olam.
Ki sheshet yamim asah adonay et hashamayim
ve'et ha'aretz
uvayom hashevi'i shavat vayinafash.

(When Shabbat coincides with a festival, add:

וַיְדַבֵּר מֹשֶׁה אֶת־מֹעֲדֵי יהוה אֶל־בְּנֵי יִשְׂרָאֵל:

Vaydaber mosheh et mo'adey adonay el beney yisra'el.)

NOTE. *Veshameru* (Exodus 31:16–17) serves as the introduction to the Amidah (silent prayer) of Shabbat eve. In places where prayerbooks were scarce, this prologue served as a reminder to include the Shabbat *beraḥah* in the silent prayer which follows. S.S.

וידבר . . . ישראל / Moses . . . Israel (Leviticus 23:44).

ḤATZI KADDISH / SHORT KADDISH

Reader: Let God's name be made great and holy in the world that was created as God willed. May God complete the holy realm in your own lifetime, in your days, and in the days of all the house of Israel, quickly and soon. And say: Amen.

Congregation: May God's great name be blessed, forever and as long as worlds endure.

Reader: May it be blessed, and praised, and glorified, and held in honor, viewed with awe, embellished, and revered; and may the blessed name of holiness be hailed, though it be higher (*On Shabbat Shuvah add:* by far) than all the blessings, songs, praises, and consolations that we utter in this world. And say: Amen.

חֲצִי קַדִּישׁ

יִתְגַּדַּל וְיִתְקַדַּשׁ שְׁמֵהּ רַבָּא בְּעָלְמָא דִּי בְרָא כִרְעוּתֵהּ וְיַמְלִיךְ מַלְכוּתֵהּ בְּחַיֵּיכוֹן וּבְיוֹמֵיכוֹן וּבְחַיֵּי דְכָל בֵּית יִשְׂרָאֵל בַּעֲגָלָא וּבִזְמַן קָרִיב וְאִמְרוּ אָמֵן:

יְהֵא שְׁמֵהּ רַבָּא מְבָרַךְ לְעָלַם וּלְעָלְמֵי עָלְמַיָּא:

יִתְבָּרַךְ וְיִשְׁתַּבַּח וְיִתְפָּאַר וְיִתְרוֹמַם וְיִתְנַשֵּׂא וְיִתְהַדָּר וְיִתְעַלֶּה וְיִתְהַלַּל שְׁמֵהּ דְּקֻדְשָׁא בְּרִיךְ הוּא

לְעֵֽלָּא (*On Shabbat Shuvah add:* לְעֵֽלָּא) מִן כָּל בִּרְכָתָא וְשִׁירָתָא תֻּשְׁבְּחָתָא וְנֶחֱמָתָא דַּאֲמִירָן בְּעָלְמָא וְאִמְרוּ אָמֵן:

Reader: Yitgadal veyitkadash shemeh raba be'alma divra ḥiruteh veyamliḥ malḥuteh beḥayeyḥon uvyomeyḥon uvḥayey deḥol beyt yisra'el ba'agala uvizman kariv ve'imru amen.

Congregation: Yehey shemeh raba mevaraḥ le'alam ulalmey almaya.

Reader: Yitbaraḥ veyishtabaḥ veyitpa'ar veyitromam veyitnasey veyit-hadar veyitaleh veyit-halal shemeh dekudsha beriḥ hu

le'ela (*On Shabbat Shuvah add:* le'ela) min kol birḥata veshirata tushbeḥata veneḥemata da'amiran be'alma ve'imru amen.

INTRODUCTIONS TO THE AMIDAH

Standing here in Abraham's desert
Affirming: one God.

Moving in the old spaces
Warmed by our ancestors' embrace.

Standing here in Sarah's tent
Laughing: new life.

Moving in the old spaces
Renewed by our ancestors' hope.

Standing here in my place
Listening to our voices: yearning.

Moving in my own spaces
Translating the silence.

Sandy Eisenberg Sasso

* *

Dear God,
Open the blocked passageways to you,
The congealed places.

Roll away the heavy stone from the well as your servant
Jacob did when he beheld his beloved Rachel.

Help us open the doors of trust that have been jammed with
hurt and rejection.

As you open the blossoms in spring,
Even as you open the heavens in storm,
Open us—to feel your great, awesome, wonderful presence.

Sheila Peltz Weinberg

KAVANAH. Prayer is communion. To commune with God is to put oneself in touch with the source of cosmic energy. M.M.K.

ואני תפלתי-לך יהוה עת רצון אלהים ברב-חסדך ענני באמת ישעך

מהללה שם יהוה ממזרח-שמש עד-מבואו

From the sun's rising to its setting the name of Yah is to be praised.

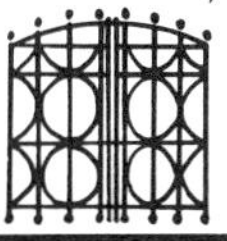

שמש וירח הללוה

Praise Yah sun and moon

שויתי יהוה לנגדי תמיד

יהיו לרצון אמרי פי והגיון לבי לפניך יהוה צורי וגאלי:

May my words of prayer and my heart's meditation be seen favorably, Yah/Beloved One, my rock and my redeemer.

כל הנשמה תהלל יה הללויה:

Let every living thing Yah's praises sing! Hallelu-Yah!

אדני שפתי תפתח ופי יגיד תהלתך

Open my lips, God, and let my mouth declare your praise.

מצות יהוה ברה מאירת עינים

יראת יהוה טהורה עומדת לעד

פתחו-לי שערי-צדק אבא-בם אודה יה

יהוה עז לעמו יתן יהוה יברך את-עמו בשלום

שמע-יהוה קולי אקרא וחנני וענני

השתחוו ליהוה בהדרת-קדש

Open the gates of righteousness for me, that I may enter & praise Yah/

Yah/the Gracious One, blessing the people in their peace

Hear, O Yah, when I cry aloud; have mercy on me, answer me

Bow down to Yah/Grandeur with holy adornment

אלהי, נשמה שנתת בי
טהורה היא. אתה בראתה,
אתה יצרתה, אתה נפחתה בי,
ואתה משמרה בקרבי, ואתה
עתיד לטלה ממני ולהחזירה
בי לעתיד לבא. כל זמן
שהנשמה בקרבי מודה אני
לפניך, יהוה.

כה-אמר האל יהוה
בורא השמים ונוטיהם רקע
הארץ וצאצאיה נתן נשמה
לעם עליה ורוח להלכים בה:
אני יהוה קראתיך בצדק
ואחזק בידך ואצרך ואתנך
לברית עם
לאור גוים:

Were our lips full of praise as the wide expanse of heaven and our eyes sparkling like the sun or the moon, were our hands spread out in prayer as the eagles of the sky, our feet swift as deer—

We could still not fully thank you...

אילו פינו מלא שירה כים ולשוננו רנה כהמון גליו ושפתותינו שבח כמרחבי רקיע ועינינו מאירות כשמש וכירח וידינו פרושות כנשרי שמים ורגלינו קלות כאילות

אין אנחנו מספיקים להודות לך

וייצר יהוה אלהים את-האדם עפר מן-האדמה ויפח באפיו נשמת חיים ויהי האדם לנפש חיה

"נשמה" בגמטריה "השמים"

AMIDAH

The traditional Amidah follows here. An interpretive Amidah begins on page 150. Directed meditations begin on page 179. A short Amidah can be found on page 184. The Amidah is traditionally recited while standing, beginning with three short steps forward while bowing, a reminder of our entry into the divine presence. For additional readings see pages 188–189, 191–194, 204–205.

Open my lips, YAH / DEAR ONE,
and let my mouth declare your praise.

1. AVOT / ANCESTORS

Blessed are you, YAH / ANCIENT ONE our God, God of our ancestors,

God of Abraham	God of Sarah
God of Isaac	God of Rebekah
God of Jacob	God of Rachel
	and God of Leah;

COMMENTARY. A. J. Heschel has said, "The term, 'God of Abraham, Isaac, and Jacob' is semantically different from a term such as 'the God of truth, goodness, and beauty.' Abraham, Isaac and Jacob do not signify ideas, principles or abstract values. Nor do they stand for teachers or thinkers, and the term is not to be understood like that of 'the God of Kant, Hegel, and Schelling.' Abraham, Isaac, and Jacob are not principles to be comprehended but lives to be continued. The life of one who joins the covenant of Abraham continues the life of Abraham. For the present is not apart from the past. 'Abraham is still standing before God' (Genesis 18:22). Abraham endures forever. We are Abraham, Isaac, and Jacob." In this same spirit, we are also Sarah and Rebekah, Rachel and Leah. L.W.K.

KAVANAH. The introductory words (Psalm 51:17) of the Amidah contain a paradox of divine and human power. Our ability to be whole, upright, free, and fully alive grows as we acknowledge and appreciate an infinitely higher source of power in the universe. This allows us to be receptive. By acknowledging our human vulnerability we open our hearts to the support, compassion, and faithfulness available around us. S.P.W.

עֲמִידָה

The traditional Amidah follows here. An interpretive Amidah begins on page 150. Directed meditations begin on page 179. A short Amidah can be found on page 184. The Amidah is traditionally recited while standing, beginning with three short steps forward while bowing, a reminder of our entry into the divine presence.

אֲדֹנָי שְׂפָתַי תִּפְתָּח וּפִי יַגִּיד תְּהִלָּתֶךָ:

א. אָבוֹת

בָּרוּךְ אַתָּה יהוה אֱלֹהֵינוּ וֵאלֹהֵי אֲבוֹתֵינוּ וְאִמּוֹתֵינוּ

אֱלֹהֵי אַבְרָהָם אֱלֹהֵי שָׂרָה
אֱלֹהֵי יִצְחָק אֱלֹהֵי רִבְקָה
אֱלֹהֵי יַעֲקֹב אֱלֹהֵי רָחֵל
וֵאלֹהֵי לֵאָה: ←

COMMENTARY. The *Tefilah,* "The Prayer," is the central prayer of the worship service. The language and manner of reciting the *Tefilah* offer insights into the place of the individual in communal prayer. When the *Tefilah* is recited privately, each individual stands (hence the name Amidah, "standing") and addresses God in a sustained conversational way. Calling God "you" indicates intimacy and immediacy. Nevertheless, the individual prays with the communal voice: "We acknowledge you," "Bless us," "Grant us peace." The Mishnah provides the structure within which additional prayers and petitions are placed. Even an individual's private needs have importance within the communal context.

Throughout the centuries the pursuit of meaningful communal prayer has led to variations in the Amidah. These variations reflect the attitudes and beliefs of different prayer communities. In the ongoing pursuit of meaningful prayer for a Reconstructionist prayer community, changes have been introduced into this Amidah, most notably in the first two of the seven *beraḥot* which comprise the Shabbat Amidah. The first *beraḥah* has been expanded to include the matriarchs along with the patriarchs as exemplars of God's presence in human lives. By concentrating on examples of healing forces and life-sustaining rains, the second *beraḥah* acknowledges God as the power that sustains life. The traditional emphasis on God's ability to resurrect the dead has been replaced here by a celebration of God as the power that sustains all life. S.S.

great, heroic, awesome God, supreme divinity,
imparting deeds of kindness, begetter of all;
mindful of the loyalty of Israel's ancestors,
bringing, with love, redemption to their children's children
for the sake of the Boundless Name.

On Shabbat Shuvah add:
(Remember us for life,
sovereign who wishes us to live,
and write us in the Book of Life,
for your sake, ever-living God.)

Regal One, our help, salvation, and protector:
Blessed are you, YAH / KIND ONE
Shield of Abraham and help of Sarah. ↵

עזרת שרה / *ezrat sarah.* The biblical term *ezer* has two meanings, "rescue" and "be strong." It is commonly translated as "aid" or "help." It also has the sense of power and strength. In Deuteronomy 33:29, *ezer* is parallel to גאוה, majesty. Eve is described as Adam's *ezer kenegdo,* a power equal to him, a strength and majesty to match his. Thus *magen avraham* (shield of Abraham) and *ezrat sarah* (help of Sarah) are parallel images of power and protection. R.A.

KAVANAH. God is experienced as עוזר, helper, every time our thought of God furnishes us an escape from the sense of frustration and supplies us with a feeling of permanence in the midst of universal flux.
M.M.K. (ADAPTED)

הָאֵל הַגָּדוֹל הַגִּבּוֹר וְהַנּוֹרָא אֵל עֶלְיוֹן גּוֹמֵל חֲסָדִים טוֹבִים וְקוֹנֵה הַכֹּל וְזוֹכֵר חַסְדֵי אָבוֹת וּמֵבִיא גְאֻלָּה לִבְנֵי בְנֵיהֶם לְמַ֫עַן שְׁמוֹ בְּאַהֲבָה:

On Shabbat Shuvah add:

(זָכְרֵ֫נוּ לְחַיִּים מֶ֫לֶךְ חָפֵץ בַּחַיִּים וְכָתְבֵ֫נוּ בְּסֵ֫פֶר הַחַיִּים לְמַעַנְךָ אֱלֹהִים חַיִּים:)

מֶ֫לֶךְ עוֹזֵר וּמוֹשִׁ֫יעַ וּמָגֵן: בָּרוּךְ אַתָּה יהוה מָגֵן אַבְרָהָם וְעֶזְרַת שָׂרָה:←

In each age
we receive and transmit
Torah.
At each moment
we are addressed by the
World.
In each age
we are challenged
by our ancient teaching.
At each moment
we stand face to Face with
Truth.
In each age
we add our wisdom
to that which has gone before.
At each moment
the knowing heart
is filled with wonder.
In each age
the children of Torah
become its builders
and seek to set the world firm
on a foundation of Truth.

R.M.S.

2. GEVUROT / DIVINE POWER

You are forever powerful, $\frac{\text{YAH}}{\text{MIGHTY ONE}}$ abundant in your saving acts.

In summer:

You send down the dew.

In winter:

You make the wind blow and rain fall.

In loyalty you sustain all the living, nurture the life of every living thing: uphold those who fall, heal the sick, free the captive, and remain faithful to all life held dormant in the earth. Who can compare to you, almighty God, who can resemble you, the source of life and death, who makes salvation grow!

(*On Shabbat Shuvah add:* Who can compare to you, source of all mercy, remembering all creatures mercifully, decreeing life!)

Faithful are you in giving life to every living thing. Blessed are you, $\frac{\text{YAH}}{\text{REVIVER}}$ who gives and renews life.

3. KEDUSHAT HASHEM / NAMING THE HOLY

Holy are you. Your name is holy. And all holy beings hail you each day. Blessed are you, $\frac{\text{YAH}}{\text{THE AWESOME ONE}}$ the holy God.כ

(*On Shabbat Shuvah conclude:* the holy monarch.)

מוריד הטל / משיב הרוח. We acknowledge the presence of God in the natural rhythms of passing seasons. Our awareness of wind, rain, and dew as daily miracles also serves to remind us that the purity of these gifts, so vital for our survival, must be maintained by human watchfulness. In thanking God for air and water, we assert our commitment to preserving

ב. גְבוּרוֹת

אַתָּה גִּבּוֹר לְעוֹלָם אֲדֹנָי רַב לְהוֹשִׁיעַ:

מוֹרִיד הַטָּל: *In summer:*

מַשִּׁיב הָרֽוּחַ וּמוֹרִיד הַגָּֽשֶׁם: *In winter:*

מְכַלְכֵּל חַיִּים בְּחֶֽסֶד מְחַיֵּה כָּל חַי בְּרַחֲמִים רַבִּים סוֹמֵךְ נוֹפְלִים וְרוֹפֵא חוֹלִים וּמַתִּיר אֲסוּרִים וּמְקַיֵּם אֱמוּנָתוֹ לִישֵׁנֵי עָפָר: מִי כָמֽוֹךָ בַּֽעַל גְּבוּרוֹת וּמִי דֽוֹמֶה לָּךְ מֶֽלֶךְ מֵמִית וּמְחַיֶּה וּמַצְמִֽיחַ יְשׁוּעָה:

On Shabbat Shuvah add:

(מִי כָמֽוֹךָ אַב הָרַחֲמִים זוֹכֵר יְצוּרָיו לְחַיִּים בְּרַחֲמִים:)

וְנֶאֱמָן אַתָּה לְהַחֲיוֹת כָּל חָי: בָּרוּךְ אַתָּה יהוה מְחַיֵּה כָּל חָי:

ג. קְדֻשַּׁת הַשֵּׁם

אַתָּה קָדוֹשׁ וְשִׁמְךָ קָדוֹשׁ וּקְדוֹשִׁים בְּכָל יוֹם יְהַלְלֽוּךָ סֶּֽלָה:
בָּרוּךְ אַתָּה יהוה הָאֵל הַקָּדוֹשׁ: ←

(הַמֶּֽלֶךְ הַקָּדוֹשׁ *On Shabbat Shuvah conclude:*)

---

them as sources of life and protecting them from life-destroying pollution. The mention of rain or dew follows the two-season climate of *Eretz Yisra'el;* summer extends from the first day of Pesaḥ until Shemini Atzeret, and winter until the following Pesaḥ. A.G.

4. KEDUSHAT HAYOM / THE DAY'S HOLINESS

You sanctified the seventh day, your signature upon completion of the heavens and the earth. You made it most blessed of all days, declared it holiest of times. Thus is it written in your Torah:

> Heaven, earth, and all their beings were finished. God completed on the seventh day the work that had been done, and ceased upon the seventh day from all the work that had been done. God blessed the seventh day and set it apart. For on it God had ceased from all the work that had been done in carrying out Creation.

Our God, our ancients' God, take pleasure in our rest. Make us holy through your mitzvot. Make us a part of Torah. Let us enjoy the good things of your world and rejoice in all your saving acts. Refine our hearts to serve you honestly. Help us to perpetuate, with love and joy, your holy Shabbat. Let all Israel, and all who treat your name as holy, rest upon this day. Blessed are you, YAH / SACRED ONE source of the holiness of Shabbat. ↵

DERASH. We ask God to remove the impurities that have collected in our minds so that we might be truthful enough to serve God. What are these impurities, these false coverings? They are the myth of isolation, the denial of interrelatedness, the prideful pretense that we are alone and abandoned in the cosmos. S.P.W.

DERASH. The creation of the world is not completed so long as we have not fulfilled our creative function in it. M.M.K.

ויכלו . . . לעשות / Heaven . . . Creation (Genesis 2:1–3).

ד. קְדֻשַּׁת הַיּוֹם

אַתָּה קִדַּשְׁתָּ אֶת יוֹם הַשְּׁבִיעִי לִשְׁמֶךָ תַּכְלִית מַעֲשֵׂה שָׁמַיִם וָאָרֶץ וּבֵרַכְתּוֹ מִכָּל הַיָּמִים וְקִדַּשְׁתּוֹ מִכָּל הַזְּמַנִּים וְכֵן כָּתוּב בְּתוֹרָתֶךָ:

וַיְכֻלּוּ הַשָּׁמַיִם וְהָאָרֶץ וְכָל־צְבָאָם: וַיְכַל אֱלֹהִים בַּיּוֹם הַשְּׁבִיעִי מְלַאכְתּוֹ אֲשֶׁר עָשָׂה וַיִּשְׁבֹּת בַּיּוֹם הַשְּׁבִיעִי מִכָּל־מְלַאכְתּוֹ אֲשֶׁר עָשָׂה: וַיְבָרֶךְ אֱלֹהִים אֶת־יוֹם הַשְּׁבִיעִי וַיְקַדֵּשׁ אֹתוֹ כִּי בוֹ שָׁבַת מִכָּל־מְלַאכְתּוֹ אֲשֶׁר־בָּרָא אֱלֹהִים לַעֲשׂוֹת:

אֱלֹהֵינוּ וֵאלֹהֵי אֲבוֹתֵינוּ וְאִמּוֹתֵינוּ רְצֵה בִמְנוּחָתֵנוּ: קַדְּשֵׁנוּ בְּמִצְוֹתֶיךָ וְתֵן חֶלְקֵנוּ בְּתוֹרָתֶךָ שַׂבְּעֵנוּ מִטּוּבֶךָ וְשַׂמְּחֵנוּ בִּישׁוּעָתֶךָ וְטַהֵר לִבֵּנוּ לְעָבְדְּךָ בֶּאֱמֶת: וְהַנְחִילֵנוּ יהוה אֱלֹהֵינוּ בְּאַהֲבָה וּבְרָצוֹן שַׁבַּת קָדְשֶׁךָ וְיָנוּחוּ בָהּ כָּל יִשְׂרָאֵל מְקַדְּשֵׁי שְׁמֶךָ: בָּרוּךְ אַתָּה יהוה מְקַדֵּשׁ הַשַּׁבָּת:←

KAVANAH. Through our observance of Shabbat, we shall come to know God as the source of salvation. In that state of being, our powers are harmoniously employed in the achievement of worthwhile aims.

M.M.K. (ADAPTED)

COMMENTARY. One of the most distinguished words in the Bible is the word *kadosh,* a word which more than any other is representative of the mystery and the majesty of the divine. Now what was the first holy object in the history of the world? Was it a mountain? Was it an altar?

It is indeed a unique occasion at which the word *kadosh* is used for the first time: in the book of Genesis, at the end of the story of creation. How extremely significant is the fact that it is applied to time. "And God blessed the seventh day and made it *kadosh.*" There is no reference in the record of creation to any object in space that would be endowed with the quality of *kedushah,* holiness.

A.J.H.

5. AVODAH / WORSHIP

Take pleasure YAH / GRACIOUS ONE our God, in Israel your people; lovingly accept their passionate prayer. May Israel's worship always be acceptable to you.

(*When Shabbat coincides with a New Moon or festival, add:* Our God, our ancients' God, may our prayer arise and come to you, and be beheld, and be acceptable. Let it be heard, acted upon, remembered—the memory of us and all our needs, the memory of our ancestors, the memory of messianic days, the memory of Jerusalem your holy city, and the memory of all your kin, the house of Israel, all surviving in your presence. Act for goodness and grace, for love and care; for life, well-being and peace, on this day of

On Rosh Ḥodesh: the new moon.
On Pesaḥ: the festival of matzot.
On Sukkot: the festival of sukkot.

KAVANAH. Prayer itself is the divinity. PINḤAS OF KORETZ

וזכרון ימות משיח צדקך. We assert our faith in the coming of a messianic age, a time when justice will reign and all humanity will be united in recognition of the one God. Even in our people's darkest hour, this vision of the future strengthened us as we faced both life and death. However distanced we may be from the more naive aspects of belief in the person of messiah, the vision of a transformed future remains our guide, just as we know that this vision will become reality only if our deeds reflect it. A.G.

ה. עֲבוֹדָה

רְצֵה יהוה אֱלֹהֵינוּ בְּעַמְּךָ יִשְׂרָאֵל וְלַהַב תְּפִלָּתָם בְּאַהֲבָה תְקַבֵּל בְּרָצוֹן וּתְהִי לְרָצוֹן תָּמִיד עֲבוֹדַת יִשְׂרָאֵל עַמֶּךָ:

When Shabbat coincides with a New Moon or Festival, add:

(אֱלֹהֵינוּ וֵאלֹהֵי אֲבוֹתֵינוּ וְאִמּוֹתֵינוּ יַעֲלֶה וְיָבוֹא וְיַגִּיעַ וְיֵרָאֶה וְיֵרָצֶה וְיִשָּׁמַע וְיִפָּקֵד וְיִזָּכֵר זִכְרוֹנֵנוּ וּפִקְדוֹנֵנוּ וְזִכְרוֹן אֲבוֹתֵינוּ וְזִכְרוֹן יְמוֹת מְשִׁיחַ צִדְקֶךָ וְזִכְרוֹן יְרוּשָׁלַיִם עִיר קָדְשֶׁךָ וְזִכְרוֹן כָּל עַמְּךָ בֵּית יִשְׂרָאֵל לְפָנֶיךָ לִפְלֵיטָה וּלְטוֹבָה לְחֵן וּלְחֶסֶד וּלְרַחֲמִים לְחַיִּים וּלְשָׁלוֹם בְּיוֹם

On Rosh Ḥodesh: רֹאשׁ הַחֹדֶשׁ הַזֶּה

On Pesaḥ: חַג הַמַּצּוֹת הַזֶּה

On Sukkot: חַג הַסֻּכּוֹת הַזֶּה

←

ולהב תפלתם. The external mouthing of words alone cannot move us. It is the inward flame of devotion that brings our prayer close to God. Indeed, as the Hebrew phrasing vividly conveys, a passionate longing for godliness can exist among those unable to express that feeling in words. The phrase *lahav tefilatam,* "the flame of Israel's prayer," recalls that feeling of *hitlahavut:* the "in-burning" flame of passionate devotion. To attain *hitlahavut* in prayer is to soar with the rapturous ecstasy of divine communion, to access the infinite and be aflame with the nearness of God.

A.G. / M.P.

Remember us this day, YAH / ALL-KNOWING our God, for goodness. Favor us this day with blessing. Preserve us this day for life. With your redeeming and nurturing word, be kind and generous. Act tenderly on our behalf, and grant us victory over all our trials. Truly, our eyes turn toward you, for you are a providing God; gracious and merciful are you.)

And may our eyes behold your homecoming, with merciful intent, to Zion. Blessed are you, YAH / THE FAITHFUL ONE who brings your presence home to Zion.

6. HODA'AH / THANKS

We give thanks to you that you are YAH / THE CAUSE OF BEING our God, God of our ancestors, today and always. A firm, enduring source of life, a shield to us in time of trial; you are ever there, from age to age. We acknowledge you, declare your praise, and thank you for our lives entrusted to your hand, our souls placed in your care, for your miracles that greet us every day, and for your wonders and the good things that are with us every hour, morning, noon, and night. Good One, whose kindness never stops, Kind One, whose loving acts have never failed—always have we placed our hope in you.

KAVANAH. So long as the Jewish people is linked in communion with the eternal, it can look forward to an eternal life for itself.

M.M.K. (ADAPTED)

KAVANAH. Gratitude is the overwhelming experience of the person of faith. Faith stimulates gratitude, and the practice of gratitude expands faith. We experience thankfulness when we know that our lives are safe within God's protection. We trust that the future is assured. We need not consume our days in fear and anxiety. We are released. We can marvel at the daily wonders. S.P.W.

זָכְרֵֽנוּ יהוה אֱלֹהֵינוּ בּוֹ לְטוֹבָה: וּפָקְדֵֽנוּ לִבְרָכָה וְהוֹשִׁיעֵֽנוּ בוֹ לְחַיִּים: וּבִדְבַר יְשׁוּעָה וְרַחֲמִים חוּס וְחָנֵּֽנוּ וְרַחֵם עָלֵֽינוּ וְהוֹשִׁיעֵֽנוּ כִּי אֵלֶֽיךָ עֵינֵֽינוּ כִּי אֵל מֶֽלֶךְ חַנּוּן וְרַחוּם אָֽתָּה:)

וְתֶחֱזֶֽינָה עֵינֵֽינוּ בְּשׁוּבְךָ לְצִיּוֹן בְּרַחֲמִים: בָּרוּךְ אַתָּה יהוה הַמַּחֲזִיר שְׁכִינָתוֹ לְצִיּוֹן:

ו. הוֹדָאָה

מוֹדִים אֲנַֽחְנוּ לָךְ שָׁאַתָּה הוּא יהוה אֱלֹהֵינוּ וֵאלֹהֵי אֲבוֹתֵֽינוּ וְאִמּוֹתֵֽינוּ לְעוֹלָם וָעֶד צוּר חַיֵּֽינוּ מָגֵן יִשְׁעֵֽנוּ אַתָּה הוּא לְדוֹר וָדוֹר: נוֹדֶה לְּךָ וּנְסַפֵּר תְּהִלָּתֶֽךָ עַל חַיֵּֽינוּ הַמְּסוּרִים בְּיָדֶֽךָ וְעַל נִשְׁמוֹתֵֽינוּ הַפְּקוּדוֹת לָךְ וְעַל נִסֶּֽיךָ שֶׁבְּכָל יוֹם עִמָּֽנוּ וְעַל נִפְלְאוֹתֶֽיךָ וְטוֹבוֹתֶֽיךָ שֶׁבְּכָל־עֵת עֶֽרֶב וָבֹֽקֶר וְצָהֳרָֽיִם: הַטּוֹב כִּי לֹא כָלוּ רַחֲמֶֽיךָ וְהַמְרַחֵם כִּי לֹא תַֽמּוּ חֲסָדֶֽיךָ מֵעוֹלָם קִוִּֽינוּ לָךְ: ←

DERASH. The insights of wonder must be constantly kept alive. Since there is a need for daily wonder, there is a need for daily worship. The sense of the "miracles which are daily with us," the sense of the "continual marvels," is the source of prayer. There is no worship, no music, no love, if we take for granted the blessings or defeats of living. . . . The profound and perpetual awareness of the wonder of being has become a part of the religious consciousness of the Jew. A.J.H.

(*On Ḥanukah add:* For the miracles, for the redemption, for heroic acts, for saving deeds, for consolations, all of which you have enacted for our ancestors at this time of year in days gone by—as in the days of Matthew, son of Yoḥanan, Hasmonean High Priest, and Matthew's sons: a wicked Hellenistic government arose against your people Israel, forcing them to shun your Torah and to leave off from the laws your will ordained. And you, in your abundant mercy, stood up for Israel in their hour of distress. You pressed their claim, exacted justice for them. You delivered armed might to the weak, the many to the power of the few, the wicked to the power of the just, the vicious to the power of those immersed in your Torah. You made known your name that day, and made it holy in your world. And for your people Israel you enacted great deliverance, as in our own time. Afterward, your children came into your Temple's inner room, cleared your sanctuary, purified your holy place, kindled lights inside your holy courtyards, and established these eight days of Ḥanukah, for giving thanks and praise to your great name.)

For all these things, let your name be blessed and raised in honor always, sovereign of ours, forever.

(*On Shabbat Shuvah add:* And write down for a good life all the people of your covenant.)

Let all of life acknowledge you! May all beings praise your name in truth, O God, our rescue and our aid. Blessed are you, YAH / GRACIOUS ONE whose name is good, to whom all thanks are due.

On Ḥanukah add:

(עַל הַנִּסִּים וְעַל הַפֻּרְקָן וְעַל הַגְּבוּרוֹת וְעַל הַתְּשׁוּעוֹת וְעַל הַנֶּחָמוֹת שֶׁעָשִׂיתָ לַאֲבוֹתֵינוּ בַּיָּמִים הָהֵם בַּזְּמַן הַזֶּה: בִּימֵי מַתִּתְיָהוּ בֶּן יוֹחָנָן כֹּהֵן גָּדוֹל חַשְׁמוֹנַאי וּבָנָיו כְּשֶׁעָמְדָה מַלְכוּת יָוָן הָרְשָׁעָה עַל עַמְּךָ יִשְׂרָאֵל לְהַשְׁכִּיחָם תּוֹרָתֶךָ וּלְהַעֲבִירָם מֵחֻקֵּי רְצוֹנֶךָ וְאַתָּה בְּרַחֲמֶיךָ הָרַבִּים עָמַדְתָּ לָהֶם בְּעֵת צָרָתָם רַבְתָּ אֶת רִיבָם דַּנְתָּ אֶת דִּינָם מָסַרְתָּ גִּבּוֹרִים בְּיַד חַלָּשִׁים וְרַבִּים בְּיַד מְעַטִּים וּרְשָׁעִים בְּיַד צַדִּיקִים וְזֵדִים בְּיַד עוֹסְקֵי תוֹרָתֶךָ: וּלְךָ עָשִׂיתָ שֵׁם גָּדוֹל וְקָדוֹשׁ בְּעוֹלָמֶךָ וּלְעַמְּךָ יִשְׂרָאֵל עָשִׂיתָ תְּשׁוּעָה גְדוֹלָה וּפֻרְקָן כְּהַיּוֹם הַזֶּה: וְאַחַר כֵּן בָּאוּ בָנֶיךָ לִדְבִיר בֵּיתֶךָ וּפִנּוּ אֶת הֵיכָלֶךָ וְטִהֲרוּ אֶת מִקְדָּשֶׁךָ וְהִדְלִיקוּ נֵרוֹת בְּחַצְרוֹת קָדְשֶׁךָ וְקָבְעוּ שְׁמוֹנַת יְמֵי חֲנֻכָּה אֵלּוּ לְהוֹדוֹת וּלְהַלֵּל לְשִׁמְךָ הַגָּדוֹל:)

וְעַל כֻּלָּם יִתְבָּרַךְ וְיִתְרוֹמַם שִׁמְךָ מַלְכֵּנוּ תָּמִיד לְעוֹלָם וָעֶד:

(וּכְתֹב לְחַיִּים טוֹבִים כָּל־בְּנֵי בְרִיתֶךָ: *On Shabbat Shuvah add:*)

וְכֹל הַחַיִּים יוֹדוּךָ סֶּלָה וִיהַלְלוּ אֶת שִׁמְךָ בֶּאֱמֶת הָאֵל יְשׁוּעָתֵנוּ וְעֶזְרָתֵנוּ סֶלָה: בָּרוּךְ אַתָּה יהוה הַטּוֹב שִׁמְךָ וּלְךָ נָאֶה לְהוֹדוֹת:←

7. BIRKAT HASHALOM / PEACE BLESSING

Grant abundant peace eternally for Israel, your people. For you are the sovereign source of all peace. So, may it be a good thing in your eyes to bless your people Israel, and all who dwell on earth, in every time and hour, with your peace.

(*On Shabbat Shuvah add:* In the book of life, blessing, peace, and proper sustenance, may we be remembered and inscribed, we and all your people, the house of Israel, for a good life and for peace.)

Blessed are you, YAH / HARMONY maker of peace.

The Amidah traditionally concludes with bowing and taking three steps back.

ואת כל יושבי תבל. According to the sages, every Amidah must conclude with a prayer for peace and an acknowledgement of God as the power that makes for peace. Inclusion of the words "and all who dwell on earth" proclaims that Israel desires the blessing of peace, not for itself alone, but for all humanity. S.S.

עושה השלום / Maker of peace. This ancient version of the prayer for peace in its most universal form was assigned in the traditional liturgy to the ten days of *teshuvah.* During the year the text read, "who blesses your people Israel with peace." In our times, when life has been transformed by the constant threat of global destruction, the need of the hour calls for the more universal form of the prayer throughout the year. A.G.

KAVANAH. God is shalom, God's name is shalom, everything is held together by shalom. ZOHAR

My God, you are *salam* peace.
Peace comes from you goes back to you.
Let us live in peace and with peace.
You are great and generous. SIDI SHEIKH MUHAMMAD AL JEMAL

ז. בִּרְכַּת הַשָּׁלוֹם

שָׁלוֹם רָב עַל יִשְׂרָאֵל עַמְּךָ תָּשִׂים לְעוֹלָם׃ כִּי אַתָּה הוּא מֶֽלֶךְ
אָדוֹן לְכָל הַשָּׁלוֹם׃ וְטוֹב בְּעֵינֶֽיךָ לְבָרֵךְ אֶת עַמְּךָ יִשְׂרָאֵל וְאֶת
כָּל־יוֹשְׁבֵי תֵבֵל בְּכָל עֵת וּבְכָל שָׁעָה בִּשְׁלוֹמֶֽךָ׃

On Shabbat Shuvah add:

(בְּסֵֽפֶר חַיִּים בְּרָכָה וְשָׁלוֹם וּפַרְנָסָה טוֹבָה נִזָּכֵר וְנִכָּתֵב לְפָנֶֽיךָ
אֲנַֽחְנוּ וְכָל עַמְּךָ בֵּית יִשְׂרָאֵל לְחַיִּים טוֹבִים וּלְשָׁלוֹם׃)

בָּרוּךְ אַתָּה יהוה עוֹשֵׂה הַשָּׁלוֹם׃ ←

Shalom rav al yisra'el ameḥa tasim le'olam.
Ki atah hu meleḥ adon leḥol hashalom.
Vetov be'eyneḥa levareḥ et ameḥa yisra'el
ve'et kol yoshvey tevel
beḥol et uvḥol sha'ah bishlomeḥa.

On Shabbat Shuvah add:

(Besefer ḥayim beraḥah veshalom ufarnasah tovah
nizaḥer venikatev lefaneḥa
anaḥnu veḥol ameḥa beyt yisra'el
leḥayim tovim ulshalom.)

Baruḥ atah adonay osey hashalom.

The Amidah traditionally concludes with bowing and taking three steps back.

ELOHAY NETZOR / A CONCLUDING MEDITATION

Dear God, protect my tongue from evil,
and my lips from telling lies.
May I turn away from evil
and do what is good in your sight.
Let me be counted among those who seek peace.
May my words of prayer
and my heart's meditation be seen favorably,
YAH / BELOVED ONE my rock and my redeemer.
May the one who creates harmony above
make peace
for us and for all Israel,
and for all who dwell on earth.
And say: Amen.

COMMENTARY. The Talmud lists examples of twelve personal meditations that could follow the Amidah. If this one does not speak to you, compose your own, or stand or sit in silent meditation. L.W.K.

NOTE. Like the opening verse of the Amidah, this prayer employs the singular and deals with the power of words. But here the concern is for words between people, not for those directed to God. Some people find it easier to talk to God than to talk to others. L.W.K.

KAVANAH. Sin is the failure to live up to the best that is in us. It means that our souls are not attuned to the divine—that we have betrayed God.
M.M.K. (ADAPTED)

יהיו . . . וגואלי / May . . . redeemer (Psalm 19:15).

אֱלֹהַי נְצוֹר

אֱלֹהַי נְצוֹר לְשׁוֹנִי מֵרָע
וּשְׂפָתַי מִדַּבֵּר מִרְמָה:

יְהִי רָצוֹן שֶׁאָסוּר מֵרָע
וְהַטּוֹב בְּעֵינֶֽיךָ אֶעֱשֶׂה
יְהִי חֶלְקִי עִם מְבַקְשֵׁי שָׁלוֹם וְרוֹדְפָיו:

יִהְיוּ לְרָצוֹן אִמְרֵי פִי
וְהֶגְיוֹן לִבִּי לְפָנֶֽיךָ
יהוה צוּרִי וְגוֹאֲלִי:

עוֹשֶׂה שָׁלוֹם בִּמְרוֹמָיו
הוּא יַעֲשֶׂה שָׁלוֹם
עָלֵֽינוּ וְעַל כָּל יִשְׂרָאֵל
וְעַל כָּל יוֹשְׁבֵי תֵבֵל
וְאִמְרוּ אָמֵן:

Yihyu leratzon imrey fi
vehegyon libi lefaneḥa
adonay tzuri vego'ali.
Oseh shalom bimromav
hu ya'aseh shalom
aleynu ve'al kol yisra'el
ve'al kol yoshvey tevel
ve'imru amen.

VAYḤULU / CREATION COMPLETED

"Heaven, earth, and all their beings were finished. God completed on the seventh day the work that had been done, and ceased upon the seventh day from all the work that had been done. God blessed the seventh day and set it apart. For on it God had ceased from all the work that had been done in carrying out Creation."

ME'EYN SHEVA / REPRISE OF THE AMIDAH

Blessed are you, YAH / ANCIENT ONE our God, God of our ancestors,

God of Abraham	God of Sarah
God of Isaac	God of Rebekah
God of Jacob	God of Rachel
	and God of Leah;

great, heroic, awesome God, supreme divinity,
who creates the heavens and the earth.

KAVANAH. Shabbat represents the affirmation that life is not vain or futile, but supremely worthwhile. M.M.K. (ADAPTED)

ויכלו . . . לעשות / Heaven . . . Creation (Genesis 2:1–3).

וַיְכֻלּוּ

וַיְכֻלּוּ הַשָּׁמַיִם וְהָאָרֶץ וְכָל־צְבָאָם: וַיְכַל אֱלֹהִים בַּיּוֹם הַשְּׁבִיעִי
מְלַאכְתּוֹ אֲשֶׁר עָשָׂה וַיִּשְׁבֹּת בַּיּוֹם הַשְּׁבִיעִי מִכָּל־מְלַאכְתּוֹ אֲשֶׁר
עָשָׂה: וַיְבָרֶךְ אֱלֹהִים אֶת־יוֹם הַשְּׁבִיעִי וַיְקַדֵּשׁ אֹתוֹ כִּי בוֹ
שָׁבַת מִכָּל־מְלַאכְתּוֹ אֲשֶׁר־בָּרָא אֱלֹהִים לַעֲשׂוֹת:

בָּרוּךְ אַתָּה יהוה אֱלֹהֵינוּ וֵאלֹהֵי אֲבוֹתֵינוּ וְאִמּוֹתֵינוּ:

אֱלֹהֵי אַבְרָהָם אֱלֹהֵי שָׂרָה
אֱלֹהֵי יִצְחָק אֱלֹהֵי רִבְקָה
אֱלֹהֵי יַעֲקֹב אֱלֹהֵי רָחֵל
וֵאלֹהֵי לֵאָה:

הָאֵל הַגָּדוֹל הַגִּבּוֹר וְהַנּוֹרָא אֵל עֶלְיוֹן קוֹנֵה שָׁמַיִם וָאָרֶץ: ←

Vayhulu hashamayim veha'aretz vehol tzeva'am
vayhal elohim bayom hashevi'i melahto asher asah
vayishbot bayom hashevi'i mikol melahto asher asah.
Vayvareh elohim et yom hashevi'i vaykadesh oto
ki vo shavat mikol melahto asher bara elohim la'asot.

Baruh atah adonay eloheynu velohey avoteynu ve'imoteynu
elohey avraham, elohey sarah
elohey yitzhak, elohey rivkah
elohey ya'akov, elohey rahel
velohey le'ah
ha'el hagadol hagibor vehanora
el elyon
koney shamayim va'aretz. ↩

Shielding our ancestors with a word,
a speech enlivening all beings,
the holy God (*On Shabbat Shuvah:* the holy Sovereign),
to whom no being can compare,
who gives this people rest upon the holy Shabbat—
yes, God is pleased to give them rest!
We stand in the divine presence, awed and trembling,
and offer up continually our thankful prayer,
our expression of praise.
God to whom all thanks are due,
the source of peace, who sanctifies Shabbat,
who blesses the seventh day
and gives rest in holiness
to a people steeped in Shabbat joy,
in memory of Creation in the beginning.

מגן אבות / *Magen Avot* summarizes the Shabbat Amidah. It refers to each of the seven blessings in order: shielding ancestors, giving life, providing holiness, ordaining Shabbat, allowing worship, inspiring thanks, blessing with peace. Perhaps once an alternative Amidah, *Magen Avot* today provides a joyous communal reprise of the themes first invoked in the privacy of the Amidah. D.A.T.

מֵעֵין שֶׁבַע

מָגֵן אָבוֹת בִּדְבָרוֹ מְחַיֵּה כֹּל חַי בְּמַאֲמָרוֹ הָאֵל (הַמֶּֽלֶךְ) הַקָּדוֹשׁ שֶׁאֵין כָּמֹֽוהוּ הַמֵּנִֽיחַ לְעַמּוֹ בְּיוֹם שַׁבַּת קָדְשׁוֹ כִּי בָם רָצָה לְהָנִֽיחַ לָהֶם: לְפָנָיו נַעֲבֹד בְּיִרְאָה וָפַֽחַד וְנוֹדֶה לִשְׁמוֹ בְּכָל יוֹם תָּמִיד מֵעֵין הַבְּרָכוֹת: אֵל הַהוֹדָאוֹת אֲדוֹן הַשָּׁלוֹם מְקַדֵּשׁ הַשַּׁבָּת וּמְבָרֵךְ שְׁבִיעִי וּמֵנִֽיחַ בִּקְדֻשָּׁה לְעַם מְדֻשְּׁנֵי־עֹֽנֶג זֵֽכֶר לְמַעֲשֵׂה בְרֵאשִׁית:

Magen avot bidvaro
meḥayey kol ḥay bema'amaro
ha'el (*On Shabbat Shuvah:* hameleḥ) hakadosh she'eyn kamohu
hameni'aḥ le'amo beyom shabbat kodsho
ki vam ratzah lehani'aḥ lahem.
Lefanav na'avod beyirah vafaḥad
venodeh lishmo beḥol yom tamid
me'eyn haberaḥot.
El hahoda'ot adon hashalom
mekadesh hashabbat umvareḥ shevi'i
umeniaḥ bikdushah le'am medusheney oneg
zeḥer lema'asey vereyshit.

TRADITIONAL VERSION

Our God, our ancients' God, take pleasure in our rest. Make us holy through your mitzvot. Make us a part of Torah. Let us enjoy the good things of your world and rejoice in all your saving acts. Refine our hearts to serve you honestly. Help us to perpetuate, with love and joy, your holy Shabbat. Let all Israel, and all who treat your name as holy, rest upon this day. Blessed are you, YAH / BELOVED ONE source of the holiness of Shabbat.

ALTERNATIVE VERSION

Shabbat of holiness, beloved and blessed,
may your glory dwell amidst the people of your holy place.
In you, our queen, we find our rest.
And in your holy mitzvot our souls rejoice.
With your goodness we are content.
In you our hearts grow pure,
and in your Shabbat rest we find true worship.
Holy Shabbat, source of blessing,
may you, too, be blessed in our rest.
And blessed are you, YAH / ETERNAL ONE who makes Shabbat holy.

שבת קדש האהובה. This original Hebrew text addresses Shabbat in feminine language, as bride and as queen. She is the subject of our affection and the source of our sustenance. We ask that her blessing dwell in our midst for peace and joy. We ask, too, that the Jewish people bless Shabbat with their love and devotion. M.P.

TRADITIONAL VERSION

אֱלֹהֵינוּ וֵאלֹהֵי אֲבוֹתֵינוּ וְאִמּוֹתֵינוּ רְצֵה בִמְנוּחָתֵנוּ קַדְּשֵׁנוּ
בְּמִצְוֹתֶיךָ וְתֵן חֶלְקֵנוּ בְּתוֹרָתֶךָ שַׂבְּעֵנוּ מִטּוּבֶךָ וְשַׂמְּחֵנוּ
בִּישׁוּעָתֶךָ וְטַהֵר לִבֵּנוּ לְעָבְדְּךָ בֶּאֱמֶת: וְהַנְחִילֵנוּ יהוה אֱלֹהֵינוּ
בְּאַהֲבָה וּבְרָצוֹן שַׁבַּת קָדְשֶׁךָ: וְיָנוּחוּ בָהּ כָּל יִשְׂרָאֵל מְקַדְּשֵׁי
שְׁמֶךָ: בָּרוּךְ אַתָּה יהוה מְקַדֵּשׁ הַשַּׁבָּת:

Eloheynu velohey avoteynu ve'imoteynu
retzey vimnuḥatenu.
Kadeshenu bemitzvoteḥa
veten ḥelkenu betorateḥa.
Sabe'enu mituveḥa
vesameḥenu bishu'ateḥa
vetaher libenu le'ovdeḥa be'emet.
Vehanḥilenu adonay eloheynu
be'ahavah uvratzon shabbat kodsheḥa
veyanuḥu vah yisra'el mekadeshey shemeḥa.
Baruḥ atah adonay mekadesh hashabbat.

ALTERNATIVE VERSION

שַׁבַּת קֹדֶשׁ הָאֲהוּבָה וְהַבְּרוּכָה
יִשְׁכּוֹן כְּבוֹדֵךְ בְּלֵב עַם מְקַדְּשֵׁךְ:
בָּךְ נִמְצָא מְנוּחָתֵנוּ
וּבְמִצְוֹת קְדֻשָּׁתֵךְ תָּגֵל נַפְשֵׁנוּ:
בְּטוּבֵךְ נִשְׂבַּע וּבָךְ יִטְהַר לִבֵּנוּ
וּבִמְנוּחָתֵךְ נָבוֹא לַעֲבוֹדַת אֱמֶת:
שַׁבַּת קֹדֶשׁ מְקוֹר הַבְּרָכָה
הִתְבָּרְכִי גַּם אַתְּ בִּמְנוּחָתֵנוּ
בָּרוּךְ אַתָּה יהוה מְקַדֵּשׁ הַשַּׁבָּת:

KADDISH TITKABAL / KADDISH FOR COMPLETING PRAYER

Reader: Let God's name be made great and holy in the world that was created as God willed. May God complete the holy realm in your own lifetime, in your days, and in the days of all the house of Israel, quickly and soon. And say: Amen.

Congregation: May God's great name be blessed, forever and as long as worlds endure.

Reader: May it be blessed, and praised, and glorified, and held in honor, viewed with awe, embellished, and revered; and may the blessed name of holiness be hailed, though it be higher (*On Shabbat Shuvah add:* by far) than all the blessings, songs, praises, and consolations that we utter in this world. And say: Amen. ↵

קַדִּישׁ תִּתְקַבַּל

יִתְגַּדַּל וְיִתְקַדַּשׁ שְׁמֵהּ רַבָּא בְּעָלְמָא דִּי בְרָא כִרְעוּתֵהּ
וְיַמְלִיךְ מַלְכוּתֵהּ בְּחַיֵּיכוֹן וּבְיוֹמֵיכוֹן וּבְחַיֵּי דְכָל בֵּית יִשְׂרָאֵל
בַּעֲגָלָא וּבִזְמַן קָרִיב וְאִמְרוּ אָמֵן:
יְהֵא שְׁמֵהּ רַבָּא מְבָרַךְ לְעָלַם וּלְעָלְמֵי עָלְמַיָּא:
יִתְבָּרַךְ וְיִשְׁתַּבַּח וְיִתְפָּאַר וְיִתְרוֹמַם וְיִתְנַשֵּׂא וְיִתְהַדַּר וְיִתְעַלֶּה
וְיִתְהַלַּל שְׁמֵהּ דְּקֻדְשָׁא בְּרִיךְ הוּא
לְעֵֽלָּא (*On Shabbat Shuvah add:* לְעֵֽלָּא) מִן כָּל בִּרְכָתָא וְשִׁירָתָא
תֻּשְׁבְּחָתָא וְנֶחֱמָתָא דַּאֲמִירָן בְּעָלְמָא וְאִמְרוּ אָמֵן: ←

Reader: Yitgadal veyitkadash shemeh raba
be'alma divra ḥiruteh veyamliḥ malḥuteh
beḥayeyḥon uvyomeyḥon uvḥayey deḥol beyt yisra'el
ba'agala uvizman kariv ve'imru amen.

Congregation: Yehey shemeh raba mevaraḥ le'alam ulalmey almaya.

Reader: Yitbaraḥ veyishtabaḥ veyitpa'ar veyitromam
veyitnasey veyit-hadar veyitaleh veyit-halal
shemeh dekudsha beriḥ hu
le'ela (*On Shabbat Shuvah add:* le'ela) min kol birḥata veshirata
tushbeḥata veneḥemata da'amiran be'alma ve'imru amen. ↵

And may the prayer and supplication of the whole house of Israel be acceptable to their creator in the heavens. And say: Amen.

May Heaven grant a universal peace, and life for us, and for all Israel. And say: Amen.

May the one who creates harmony above make peace for us and for all Israel, and for all who dwell on earth. And say: Amen.

KAVANAH. Adding the rabbinic phrase "*ve'al kol yoshvey tevel*" (and for all who dwell on earth) logically completes the concentric circles of our aspirations—our care starts with our minyan, extends to the entire Jewish people, and radiates outward from there to all who share our planet.

D.A.T.

תִּתְקַבַּל צְלוֹתְהוֹן וּבָעוּתְהוֹן דְּכָל בֵּית יִשְׂרָאֵל קֳדָם אֲבוּהוֹן דִּי בִשְׁמַיָּא וְאִמְרוּ אָמֵן:

יְהֵא שְׁלָמָא רַבָּא מִן שְׁמַיָּא וְחַיִּים עָלֵינוּ וְעַל כָּל יִשְׂרָאֵל וְאִמְרוּ אָמֵן:

עוֹשֶׂה שָׁלוֹם בִּמְרוֹמָיו הוּא יַעֲשֶׂה שָׁלוֹם עָלֵינוּ וְעַל כָּל יִשְׂרָאֵל וְעַל כָּל יוֹשְׁבֵי תֵבֵל וְאִמְרוּ אָמֵן:

Titkabal tzelot-hon uva'ut-hon deḥol beyt yisra'el kodam avuhon di vishmaya ve'imru amen.

Yehey shelama raba min shemaya veḥayim aleynu ve'al kol yisra'el ve'imru amen.

Oseh shalom bimromav hu ya'aseh shalom aleynu ve'al kol yisra'el ve'al kol yoshvey tevel ve'imru amen.

Kiddush

We rise for Kiddush.

The commandment to bless this wine is a commandment to drink life as deeply as we drink from this cup.

It is a commandment to bless life and to love deeply.

It is a commandment to remember with Shabbat heart,
to act with Shabbat hands,
to see the world with Shabbat eyes.

It is a commandment to laugh until we are all laughter,
to sing until we are all song,
to dance until we are all dance,
to love until we are all love.

This is the wine that God has commanded us to bless and drink.

Sandy Eisenberg Sasso

*   *

With the permission of this company:

Blessed are you, YAH / THE BOUNDLESS ONE our God, sovereign of all worlds, who creates the fruit of the vine.

קִדּוּשׁ

We rise for Kiddush.

סָבְרֵי חֲבֵרַי:

בָּרוּךְ אַתָּה יהוה אֱלֹהֵינוּ מֶלֶךְ הָעוֹלָם בּוֹרֵא פְּרִי הַגָּפֶן: ←

Savrey ḥaveray.

Baruḥ atah adonay eloheynu meleḥ ha'olam borey peri hagafen.

COMMENTARY. The Kiddush recalls two reasons for the celebration of Shabbat—the rhythm of creation, when God rested on the seventh day; and the going forth from Egypt, when human observance of Shabbat began. Shabbat is part of nature and of history, of the cycle and the unfolding of time. The Kiddush thus illustrates how Jews discover the essence of nature through their experience of history. D.A.T.

NOTE. Hillel and Shammai argued about the order of the two blessings that comprise the Kiddush. Shammai held that the blessing of the day should come first because God ordained Kiddush as part of the order of the universe. Hillel claimed that the blessing over wine must come first because only when we taste the wine do we really begin to experience Shabbat. We follow the school of Hillel, for the metaphysical reality of Shabbat only becomes significant when we take it into ourselves. D.A.T.

Blessed are you, YAH / SOURCE OF LIFE our God, sovereign of all worlds, who has set us apart with your mitzvot and taken pleasure in us, and the holy Shabbat with love and favor made our possession, a remembrance of the work of Creation. For it is the first of all the holy days proclaimed, a symbol of the Exodus from Egypt. For you have called to us and set us apart to serve you, and given us to keep in love and favor, your holy Shabbat. Blessed are you, YAH / SOURCE OF WONDER who sets apart Shabbat.

כי אלינו קראת / for you have called to us. The traditional Ashkenazi Kiddush refers to the chosenness of the Jewish people here (כִּי בָנוּ בָחַרְתָּ / *ki vanu vaḥarta* / for you have chosen us). Reconstructionists have traditionally omitted this phrase. The 1945 Reconstructionist prayerbook substituted כִּי אוֹתָנוּ קֵרַבְתָּ לַעֲבוֹדָתֶךָ / *ki otanu keravta la'avodateḥa* / for you have drawn us near to your service. While the Ashkenazi version was rejected because of the chauvinism and triumphalism it has often sheltered, the 1945 Reconstructionist substitute neither deals with the issue of holiness as voiced in the traditional version (*ki otanu kidashta*), nor lends itself easily to song. The version used here imagines a God who calls all humanity and makes holy those who, like Israel, heed the call and engage in God's service. In this way biblical phrasing, Reconstructionist theology, and the search for holiness are seamlessly joined. D.A.T.

בָּרוּךְ אַתָּה יהוה אֱלֹהֵינוּ מֶלֶךְ הָעוֹלָם אֲשֶׁר קִדְּשָׁנוּ בְּמִצְוֹתָיו
וְרָצָה בָנוּ וְשַׁבָּת קָדְשׁוֹ בְּאַהֲבָה וּבְרָצוֹן הִנְחִילָנוּ זִכָּרוֹן לְמַעֲשֵׂה
בְרֵאשִׁית: כִּי הוּא יוֹם תְּחִלָּה לְמִקְרָאֵי קֹדֶשׁ זֵכֶר לִיצִיאַת
מִצְרָיִם: כִּי אֵלֵינוּ קָרָאתָ וְאוֹתָנוּ קִדַּשְׁתָּ לַעֲבוֹדָתֶךָ וְשַׁבַּת
קָדְשְׁךָ בְּאַהֲבָה וּבְרָצוֹן הִנְחַלְתָּנוּ: בָּרוּךְ אַתָּה יהוה מְקַדֵּשׁ
הַשַּׁבָּת:

Baruḥ atah adonay eloheynu meleḥ ha'olam
asher kideshanu bemitzvotav veratzah vanu
veshabbat kodsho be'ahavah uvratzon hinḥilanu
zikaron lema'asey vereshit.
Ki hu yom teḥilah lemikra'ey kodesh
zeḥer litzi'at mitzrayim.
Ki eleynu karata ve'otanu kidashta la'avodateḥa
veshabbat kodsheḥa be'ahavah uvratzon hinḥaltanu.
Baruḥ atah adonay mekadesh hashabbat.

ALEYNU

We rise for Aleynu. *It is customary to bow at "bend the knee." For Alternative Version see page 136. For additional readings see pages 188–190, 202–203, 205.*

It is up to us to sing the praises
of the Source of all,
to recognize the greatness
of the author of Creation,
who gave to us teachings of truth
and planted eternal life within us. ↵

COMMENTARY. The theme of *Aleynu* is the anticipation of God's universal rulership. Originally, this glorious hymn introduced the "Rulership" section of the Rosh Hashanah liturgy. Because of its lofty language and message, *Aleynu* was soon added to every worship service. The Reconstructionist version of *Aleynu* shifts the focus from a concern with the specialness of the Jewish people to an emphasis on the unique Torah perspective that enables Israel to help spread God's presence through the universe. This shift eliminates an opportunity for supporting Jewish triumphalism, in favor of stressing the importance of Torah in Jewish living. S.S.

COMMENTARY. This siddur offers, on the facing page, two additional versions of the *Aleynu*. For some Jews, the Holocaust and its aftermath have lent renewed meaning to the traditional text. Even if our lot has been that of victim, we thank God for not having made us like our persecutors. This reading also serves as a reminder that the Jewish people—now a powerful player on the scene of world history—must be on guard to avoid becoming like those nations who have done so much harm. Others still find the *Aleynu* text in need of change. The new (alternative) version offered here acknowledges the real differences between nations yet expresses faith that all who follow the path of moral goodness are doing the bidding of God.

עָלֵינוּ

We rise for Aleynu. *It is customary to bow at* "korim."

עָלֵינוּ לְשַׁבֵּחַ לַאֲדוֹן הַכֹּל לָתֵת גְּדֻלָּה לְיוֹצֵר בְּרֵאשִׁית שֶׁנָּתַן לָנוּ
תּוֹרַת אֱמֶת וְחַיֵּי עוֹלָם נָטַע בְּתוֹכֵנוּ: ←

Aleynu leshabe'aḥ la'adon hakol latet gedula leyotzer bereyshit
shenatan lanu torat emet veḥayey olam nata betohenu. ↩

Both versions begin with עָלֵינוּ לְשַׁבֵּחַ לַאֲדוֹן הַכֹּל לָתֵת גְּדֻלָּה לְיוֹצֵר בְּרֵאשִׁית / It is up to us to sing the praises of the Source of all, to recognize the greatness of the author of Creation. They then continue:

TRADITIONAL VERSION

שֶׁלֹּא עָשָׂנוּ כְּגוֹיֵי הָאֲרָצוֹת וְלֹא שָׂמָנוּ כְּמִשְׁפְּחוֹת הָאֲדָמָה שֶׁלֹּא שָׂם חֶלְקֵנוּ כָּהֶם וְגוֹרָלֵנוּ כְּכָל הֲמוֹנָם:

who has made us different from the other nations of the earth, and situated us in quite a different spot, and made our daily lot another kind from theirs, and given us a destiny uncommon in this world.

ALTERNATIVE VERSION

שֶׁעָשָׂה בְּעוֹלָמוֹ לְשׁוֹנוֹת וְעַמִּים דַּעַת דְּרָכָיו חוֹנֵן לְכֻלָּם: עַמִּים עוֹשֵׂי חֶסֶד וּבָרָע מוֹאֲסִים בִּלְשׁוֹנָם יִקְרָאוּהוּ וְיִשְׁמַע שַׁוְעָתָם:

who has made the world a web of languages and peoples, endowing all of them with the ability to know God's ways. And when they act in kindness, and turn away from cruelty, and call to God in their own tongues, God listens to their prayer. A.G.

Both versions continue with . . . ואנחנו כורעים / And so we bend the knee. . . .

And so, we bend the knee and bow,
acknowledging the sovereign who rules
above all those who rule, the blessed Holy One,
who stretched out the heavens and founded the earth,
whose realm embraces heaven's heights,
whose mighty presence stalks celestial ramparts.
This is our God; there is none else besides,
as it is written in the Torah:
"You shall know this day, and bring it home
inside your heart, that YAH / THE ULTIMATE is God
in the heavens above and on the earth below.
There is no other God." ↩

DERASH. Every person and people that feel they have something to live for, and that are bent on living that life in righteousness, are true witnesses of God. M.M.K.

KAVANAH. As the hand held before the eye hides the tallest mountain, so this small earthly life hides from our gaze the vast radiance and secrets of which the world is full, and if we can take life from before our eyes, as one takes away one's hand, we will see the great radiance within the world.
M.B. (ADAPTED)

וידעת . . . עוד /You . . . other God (Deuteronomy 4:39).

וַאֲנַֽחְנוּ כּוֹרְעִים וּמִשְׁתַּחֲוִים וּמוֹדִים לִפְנֵי מֶֽלֶךְ מַלְכֵי הַמְּלָכִים
הַקָּדוֹשׁ בָּרוּךְ הוּא:
שֶׁהוּא נוֹטֶה שָׁמַֽיִם וְיוֹסֵד אָֽרֶץ וּמוֹשַׁב יְקָרוֹ בַּשָּׁמַֽיִם מִמַּֽעַל
וּשְׁכִינַת עֻזּוֹ בְּגָבְהֵי מְרוֹמִים: הוּא אֱלֹהֵֽינוּ אֵין עוֹד: אֱמֶת
מַלְכֵּֽנוּ אֶֽפֶס זוּלָתוֹ כַּכָּתוּב בְּתוֹרָתוֹ: וְיָדַעְתָּ הַיּוֹם וַהֲשֵׁבֹתָ אֶל
לְבָבֶֽךָ כִּי יהוה הוּא הָאֱלֹהִים בַּשָּׁמַֽיִם מִמַּֽעַל וְעַל הָאָֽרֶץ מִתָּֽחַת
אֵין עוֹד: ←

Va'anaḥnu korim umishtaḥavim umodim
lifney meleḥ malḥey hamelaḥim hakadosh baruḥ hu.

Shehu noteh shamayim veyosed aretz umoshav yekaro
bashamayim mima'al
ush-ḥinat uzo begovhey meromim.
Hu eloheynu eyn od.
Emet malkenu efes zulato kakatuv betorato.
Veyadata hayom vahashevota el levaveḥa
ki adonay hu ha'elohim bashamayim mima'al ve'al ha'aretz
mitaḥat
eyn od. ↵

And so, we put our hope in you,
YAH / THE EMINENCE our God,
that soon we may behold
the full splendor of your might,
and see idolatry vanish from the earth,
and all material gods be swept away,
and the power of your rule repair the world,
and all creatures of flesh call on your name,
and all the wicked of the earth turn back to you.
Let all who dwell upon the globe perceive and know
that to you each knee must bend, each tongue swear oath,
and let them give the glory of your name its precious due.
Let all of them take upon themselves your rule.
Reign over them, soon and for always.
For this is all your realm, throughout all worlds, across all time—
as it is written in your Torah:
"YAH / THE ETERNAL ONE will reign now and forever."

And it is written:
"YAH / THE EVERLASTING ONE will reign
as sovereign over all the earth.
On that day shall YAH / THE BOUNTIFUL be one,
God's name be one!"

KAVANAH. A world of God callers is a world of truth and peace, a world where the lust for power, greed, and envy—the idols of pride—is uprooted from the individual and group psyche. S.P.W.

עַל כֵּן נְקַוֶּה לְּךָ יהוה אֱלֹהֵינוּ לִרְאוֹת מְהֵרָה בְּתִפְאֶרֶת עֻזֶּךָ לְהַעֲבִיר גִּלּוּלִים מִן הָאָרֶץ וְהָאֱלִילִים כָּרוֹת יִכָּרֵתוּן לְתַקֵּן עוֹלָם בְּמַלְכוּת שַׁדַּי: וְכָל בְּנֵי בָשָׂר יִקְרְאוּ בִשְׁמֶךָ: לְהַפְנוֹת אֵלֶיךָ כָּל רִשְׁעֵי אָרֶץ: יַכִּירוּ וְיֵדְעוּ כָּל יוֹשְׁבֵי תֵבֵל כִּי לְךָ תִּכְרַע כָּל בֶּרֶךְ תִּשָּׁבַע כָּל־לָשׁוֹן: לְפָנֶיךָ יהוה אֱלֹהֵינוּ יִכְרְעוּ וְיִפֹּלוּ וְלִכְבוֹד שִׁמְךָ יְקָר יִתֵּנוּ וִיקַבְּלוּ כֻלָּם אֶת עֹל מַלְכוּתֶךָ וְתִמְלֹךְ עֲלֵיהֶם מְהֵרָה לְעוֹלָם וָעֶד: כִּי הַמַּלְכוּת שֶׁלְּךָ הִיא וּלְעוֹלְמֵי עַד תִּמְלֹךְ בְּכָבוֹד כַּכָּתוּב בְּתוֹרָתֶךָ: יהוה יִמְלֹךְ לְעֹלָם וָעֶד: וְנֶאֱמַר: וְהָיָה יהוה לְמֶלֶךְ עַל כָּל הָאָרֶץ בַּיּוֹם הַהוּא יִהְיֶה יהוה אֶחָד וּשְׁמוֹ אֶחָד:

Kakatuv betorateḥa: Adonay yimloḥ le'olam va'ed.
Vene'emar: Vehayah adonay lemeleḥ al kol ha'aretz.
Bayom hahu yihyeh adonay eḥad ushmo eḥad.

DERASH. When senseless hatred reigns on earth and people hide their faces from one another, then heaven is forced to hide its face. But when love comes to rule the earth and people reveal their faces to one another, then the splendor of God will be revealed. M.B. (ADAPTED)

DERASH. It is not the seeking after God that divides but the claim to have found God and to have discovered the only proper way of obeying God and communing with God. M.M.K. (ADAPTED)

יהוה . . . ועד / YAH / THE ETERNAL ONE . . . forever (Exodus 15:18).

והיה . . . אחד / YAH / THE EVERLASTING ONE . . . one (Zachariah 14:9).

ALTERNATIVE VERSION

It is up to us
to hallow Creation,
to respond to Life
with the fullness of our lives.
It is up to us
to meet the World,
to embrace the Whole
even as we wrestle
with its parts.
It is up to us
to repair the World
and to bind our lives to Truth.

Therefore we bend the knee
and shake off the stiffness that keeps us
from the subtle
graces of Life
and the supple
gestures of Love.
With reverence
and thanksgiving
we accept our destiny
and set for ourselves
the task of redemption.

Rami M. Shapiro

*   *

And then all that has divided us will merge
And then compassion will be wedded to power
And then softness will come to a world that is harsh and unkind
And then both men and women will be gentle
And then both women and men will be strong
And then no person will be subject to another's will
And then all will be rich and free and varied
And then the greed of some will give way to the needs of many
And then all will share equally in the Earth's abundance
And then all will care for the sick and the weak and the old
And then all will nourish the young
And then all will cherish life's creatures
And then all will live in harmony with each other and the Earth
And then everywhere will be called Eden once again.

Judy Chicago

It is customary to acknowledge mourners on the Shabbat during Shiva, traditionally their first return to the synagogue following the death of their loved one. They are welcomed with the words:

May God console you among the mourners of Zion and Jerusalem.

THE MOURNERS' KADDISH

It is customary for mourners, and those observing Yahrzeit, to stand for Kaddish. In some congregations everyone rises. *For additional readings see pages 206–211.*

Reader: Let God's name be made great and holy in the world that was created as God willed. May God complete the holy realm in your own lifetime, in your days, and in the days of all the house of Israel, quickly and soon. And say: Amen.

Congregation: May God's great name be blessed, forever and as long as worlds endure.

It is customary to acknowledge mourners on the Shabbat during Shiva, traditionally their first return to the synagogue, following the death of their loved one. They are welcomed with the words:

הַמָּקוֹם יְנַחֵם אֶתְכֶם בְּתוֹךְ שְׁאָר אֲבֵלֵי צִיּוֹן וִירוּשָׁלָיִם:

קַדִּישׁ יָתוֹם

It is customary for mourners, and those observing Yahrzeit, to stand for Kaddish. In some congregations everyone rises.

יִתְגַּדַּל וְיִתְקַדַּשׁ שְׁמֵהּ רַבָּא בְּעָלְמָא דִּי בְרָא כִרְעוּתֵהּ
וְיַמְלִיךְ מַלְכוּתֵהּ בְּחַיֵּיכוֹן וּבְיוֹמֵיכוֹן וּבְחַיֵּי דְכָל בֵּית יִשְׂרָאֵל
בַּעֲגָלָא וּבִזְמַן קָרִיב וְאִמְרוּ אָמֵן:
יְהֵא שְׁמֵהּ רַבָּא מְבָרַךְ לְעָלַם וּלְעָלְמֵי עָלְמַיָּא: ←

Reader: Yitgadal veyitkadash shemeh raba
be'alma divra ḥiruteh veyamliḥ malḥuteh
beḥayeyḥon uvyomeyḥon uvḥayey deḥol beyt yisra'el
ba'agala uvizman kariv ve'imru amen.

Congregation: Yehey shemeh raba mevarah le'alam ulalmey almaya. ↵

Reader: May it be blessed, and praised, and glorified, and held in honor, viewed with awe, embellished, and revered; and may the blessed name of holiness be hailed, though it be higher (*On Shabbat Shuvah add:* by far) than all the blessings, songs, praises, and consolations that we utter in this world. And say: Amen.

May Heaven grant a universal peace, and life for us, and for all Israel. And say: Amen.

May the one who creates harmony above, make peace for us and for all Israel, and for all who dwell on earth. And say: Amen.

During the month of Elul, many congregations sing Aḥat Sha'alti, page 219.

יִתְבָּרַךְ וְיִשְׁתַּבַּח וְיִתְפָּאַר וְיִתְרוֹמַם וְיִתְנַשֵּׂא וְיִתְהַדַּר וְיִתְעַלֶּה וְיִתְהַלַּל שְׁמֵהּ דְּקֻדְשָׁא בְּרִיךְ הוּא
לְעֵֽלָּא (*On Shabbat Shuvah add:* לְעֵֽלָּא) מִן כָּל בִּרְכָתָא וְשִׁירָתָא תֻּשְׁבְּחָתָא וְנֶחֱמָתָא דַּאֲמִירָן בְּעָלְמָא וְאִמְרוּ אָמֵן:
יְהֵא שְׁלָמָא רַבָּא מִן שְׁמַיָּא וְחַיִּים עָלֵֽינוּ וְעַל כָּל יִשְׂרָאֵל וְאִמְרוּ אָמֵן:
עוֹשֶׂה שָׁלוֹם בִּמְרוֹמָיו הוּא יַעֲשֶׂה שָׁלוֹם עָלֵֽינוּ וְעַל כָּל יִשְׂרָאֵל וְעַל כָּל יוֹשְׁבֵי תֵבֵל וְאִמְרוּ אָמֵן:

Reader: Yitbaraḥ veyishtabaḥ veyitpa'ar veyitromam
veyitnasey veyit-hadar veyitaleh veyit-halal
shemeh dekudsha beriḥ hu
le'ela (*On Shabbat Shuvah add:* le'ela) min kol birḥata veshirata
tushbeḥata veneḥemata da'amiran be'alma ve'imru amen.

Yehey shelama raba min shemaya veḥayim aleynu ve'al kol
yisra'el ve'imru amen.
Oseh shalom bimromav hu ya'aseh shalom aleynu ve'al kol yisra'el ve'al kol yoshvey tevel ve'imru amen.

During the month of Elul, many congregations sing Aḥat Sha'alti, page 219.

ADON OLAM / CROWN OF ALL TIME

This translation can be sung to the same melody as the Hebrew.

Crown of all time, the one who reigned
before all mortal shape was made,
and when God's will brought forth all things
then was the name supreme proclaimed.

And after everything is gone,
yet One alone, awesome, will reign.
God was, and is, and will remain,
in splendid balance, over all.

And God is One, no second is,
none can compare, or share God's place.
Without beginning, without end,
God's is all might and royal grace.

This is my God, my help who lives,
refuge from pain in time of trial,
my banner, and my place to fly,
my cup's portion when, dry, I cry.

To God's kind hand I pledge my soul
each time I sleep, again to wake,
and with my soul, this body, here.
Yah's love is mine; I shall not fear.

KAVANAH. God is that aspect of reality which elicits from us the best that is in us and enables us to bear the worst that can befall us. M.M.K.

אֲדוֹן עוֹלָם

אֲדוֹן עוֹלָם אֲשֶׁר מָלַךְ   בְּטֶרֶם כָּל יְצִיר נִבְרָא:
לְעֵת נַעֲשָׂה בְחֶפְצוֹ כֹּל   אֲזַי מֶלֶךְ שְׁמוֹ נִקְרָא:
וְאַחֲרֵי כִּכְלוֹת הַכֹּל   לְבַדּוֹ יִמְלֹךְ נוֹרָא:
וְהוּא הָיָה וְהוּא הֹוֶה   וְהוּא יִהְיֶה בְּתִפְאָרָה:
וְהוּא אֶחָד וְאֵין שֵׁנִי   לְהַמְשִׁיל לוֹ לְהַחְבִּירָה:
בְּלִי רֵאשִׁית בְּלִי תַכְלִית   וְלוֹ הָעֹז וְהַמִּשְׂרָה:
וְהוּא אֵלִי וְחַי גּוֹאֲלִי   וְצוּר חֶבְלִי בְּעֵת צָרָה:
וְהוּא נִסִּי וּמָנוֹס לִי   מְנָת כּוֹסִי בְּיוֹם אֶקְרָא:
בְּיָדוֹ אַפְקִיד רוּחִי   בְּעֵת אִישַׁן וְאָעִירָה:
וְעִם רוּחִי גְּוִיָּתִי   יהוה לִי וְלֹא אִירָא:

Adon olam asher malaḥ, beterem kol yetzir nivra.
Le'et na'asah veḥeftzo kol, azay meleḥ shemo nikra.
Ve'aḥarey kiḥlot hakol, levado yimloḥ nora.
Vehu hayah vehu hoveh, vehu yihyeh betifarah.
Vehu eḥad ve'eyn sheni, lehamshil lo lehaḥbirah.
Beli reshit beli taḥlit, velo ha'oz vehamisrah.
Vehu eli veḥay go'ali, vetzur ḥevli be'et tzarah.
Vehu nisi umanos li, menat kosi beyom ekra.
Beyado afkid ruhi, be'et ishan ve'a'irah.
Ve'im ruḥi geviyati, adonay li velo ira.

YIGDAL / GREAT IS . . .

This translation can be sung to the same melody as the Hebrew.

Great is the living God,
   to whom we give our praise,
who is, and whose great being
   is timeless, without days,
the One, to whom in oneness
   no one can compare,
invisible, in unity
   unbounded, everywhere,

Who has no body's form,
   has no material dress,
nor can we find the likeness
   of God's awesome holiness,
more ancient than all things
   brought forth in creation,
the first of everything that is,
   Beginning unbegun!

Behold the supreme being,
   whose universal power,
whose greatness and whose rule
   all creatures shall declare,
whose flow of prophecy
   was granted to a few,
the treasured ones who stood amid
   God's splendor ever new. ↩

יִגְדַּל

יִגְדַּל אֱלֹהִים חַי וְיִשְׁתַּבַּח נִמְצָא וְאֵין עֵת אֶל מְצִיאוּתוֹ:
אֶחָד וְאֵין יָחִיד כְּיִחוּדוֹ נֶעְלָם וְגַם אֵין סוֹף לְאַחְדוּתוֹ:
אֵין לוֹ דְּמוּת הַגּוּף וְאֵינוֹ גוּף לֹא נַעֲרוֹךְ אֵלָיו קְדֻשָּׁתוֹ:
קַדְמוֹן לְכָל דָּבָר אֲשֶׁר נִבְרָא רִאשׁוֹן וְאֵין רֵאשִׁית לְרֵאשִׁיתוֹ:
הִנּוֹ אֲדוֹן עוֹלָם וְכָל נוֹצָר יוֹרֶה גְדֻלָּתוֹ וּמַלְכוּתוֹ:
שֶׁפַע נְבוּאָתוֹ נְתָנוֹ אֶל אַנְשֵׁי סְגֻלָּתוֹ וְתִפְאַרְתּוֹ: ←

Yigdal elohim ḥay veyishtabaḥ, nimtza ve'eyn et el metzi'uto.
Eḥad ve'eyn yaḥid keyiḥudo, nelam vegam eyn sof le'aḥduto.
Eyn lo demut haguf ve'eyno guf, lo na'aroḥ elav kedushato.
Kadmon leḥol davar asher nivra, rishon ve'eyn reyshit lereyshito.
Hino adon olam veḥol notzar, yoreh gedulato umalḥuto.
Shefa nevu'ato netano el, anshey segulato vetifar-to. ↩

NOTE. *Yigdal* was written by Daniel ben Judah, a fourteenth century poet. He based it upon Maimonides's Thirteen Articles of Faith. We have attempted to make the closing line more acceptable to the contemporary worshipper by referring to the sustenance of life, rather than resurrection of the dead, as the true testimony of God's blessing. A.G.

In Israel none arose
  as prophet like Moshe,
a prophet who would come to see
  the "image" in the *sneh.*
Torah of truth God gave
  the people Isra'el,
by truest prophet's hand
  that in God's house would dwell.

And God will never let
  the Torah pass away,
its doctrine will not change,
  but through all change will stay.
God sees and knows all things,
  and even what we hide,
can look upon how things begin
  the end of things to find,

Rewarding acts of love,
  when love for love we'll find,
and paying to all wickedness
  a recompense in kind,
God shall deliver all,
  upon the end of time,
redeeming all who wait for God,
  who for salvation pine.

God wakes all beings to life,
  abundant love shall reign,
blessed evermore,
  the glory of God's Name!

לֹא קָם בְּיִשְׂרָאֵל כְּמֹשֶׁה עוֹד נָבִיא וּמַבִּיט אֶת תְּמוּנָתוֹ:
תּוֹרַת אֱמֶת נָתַן לְעַמּוֹ אֵל עַל יַד נְבִיאוֹ נֶאֱמַן בֵּיתוֹ:
לֹא יַחֲלִיף הָאֵל וְלֹא יָמִיר דָּתוֹ לְעוֹלָמִים לְזוּלָתוֹ:
צוֹפֶה וְיוֹדֵעַ סְתָרֵינוּ מַבִּיט לְסוֹף דָּבָר בְּקַדְמָתוֹ:
גּוֹמֵל לְאִישׁ חֶסֶד כְּמִפְעָלוֹ יִתֵּן לְרָשָׁע רָע כְּרִשְׁעָתוֹ:
יִשְׁלַח לְקֵץ יָמִין גְּאֻלָּתוֹ לִפְדּוֹת מְחַכֵּי קֵץ יְשׁוּעָתוֹ:
חַיִּים מְכַלְכֵּל אֵל בְּרֹב חַסְדּוֹ בָּרוּךְ עֲדֵי עַד שֵׁם תְּהִלָּתוֹ:

Lo kam beyisra'el kemosheh od, navi umabit et temunato.
Torat emet natan le'amo el, al yad nevi'o ne'eman beyto.
Lo yaḥalif ha'el velo yamir, dato le'olamim lezulato.
Tzofeh veyode'a setareynu, mabit lesof davar bekadmato.
Gomel le'ish ḥesed kemifalo, yiten lerasha ra kerishato.
Yishlaḥ leketz yamin ge'ulato, lifdot meḥakey ketz yeshu'ato.
Ḥayim meḥalkel el berov ḥasdo, baruḥ adey ad shem tehilato.

PSALM 150

Hallelu/Yah!
Call out to Yah in Heaven's holy place!
Boom out to Yah across the firmament!
Shout out for Yah, for all God's mighty deeds!
Cry out for Yah, as loud as God is great!
Blast out for Yah with piercing *shofar* note!
Pluck out for Yah with lute and violin!
Throb out for Yah with drum and writhing dance!
Sing out for Yah with strings and husky flute!
Ring out for Yah with cymbals that resound!
Clang out for Yah with cymbals that rebound!
Let every living thing
Yah's praises sing,
Hallelu/Yah!

כֹּל הַנְּשָׁמָה תְּהַלֵּל יָהּ הַלְלוּיָהּ

Let every
living thing
Yah's praises sing!

Hallelu/Yah!

כֹּל הַנְּשָׁמָה תְּהַלֵּל יָהּ הַלְלוּיָהּ

הַלְלוּיָהּ הַלְלוּ אֵל בְּקָדְשׁוֹ הַלְלוּהוּ בִּרְקִיעַ עֻזּוֹ:
הַלְלוּהוּ בִגְבוּרֹתָיו הַלְלוּהוּ כְּרֹב גֻּדְלוֹ:
הַלְלוּהוּ בְּתֵקַע שׁוֹפָר הַלְלוּהוּ בְּנֵבֶל וְכִנּוֹר:
הַלְלוּהוּ בְּתֹף וּמָחוֹל הַלְלוּהוּ בְּמִנִּים וְעֻגָב:
הַלְלוּהוּ בְצִלְצְלֵי שָׁמַע הַלְלוּהוּ בְּצִלְצְלֵי תְרוּעָה:
כֹּל הַנְּשָׁמָה תְּהַלֵּל יָהּ הַלְלוּיָהּ:

Halleluyah halelu el bekodsho.
Haleluhu birki'a uzo.
Haleluhu vigvurotav.
Haleluhu kerov gudlo.
Haleluhu beteka shofar.
Haleluhu benevel veḥinor.
Haleluhu betof umaḥol.
Haleluhu beminim ve'ugav.
Haleluhu betziltzeley shama.
Haleluhu betziltzeley teru'ah.
Kol haneshamah tehalel yah. Halleluyah.

INTERPRETIVE AMIDAH

עֲמִידָה

תְּפִלַּת שֶׁבַע עַרְבִית לְשַׁבָּת

A SEVEN-FOLD PRAYER OF
BLESSINGS, POEMS, AND MEDITATIONS
FOR SHABBAT EVE

AUTHOR'S NOTE. This reconstruction of the Amidah prayer expresses an inclusive feminist approach to the themes of the service for Shabbat eve. Composed of women's words, it is intended for those women and men who seek to go beyond the gender limitations and hierarchical theology of the traditional siddur.

Like the traditional Hebrew Amidah, this prayer contains seven sections. Each section revaluates and reconstructs its counterpart in the traditional prayer. Thus, for example, while the first blessing of the traditional Amidah focuses on the "God of our forefathers, shield of Abraham," the first section of this new Amidah emphasizes our relationship to our ancestors—both distant and close—and to historical tradition. Malka Heifetz Tussman's poem *Ikh Bin Froi* ("I Am Woman") focuses specifically on the history of Jewish women, a subject that has been much neglected in our liturgy and teachings.

Another section of this new Amidah restores the reference to death found in the second blessing of the traditional Amidah. This restoration is based on the belief that *teḥiyat hametim* (revival of the dead) can be revaluated in a way that acknowledges and *affirms* the presence of death in our lives. Thus, the second section of this Amidah focuses on the relationship of death and dying to all life.

Each section of this Amidah comprises opening and closing lines in Hebrew and English; a *kavanah* (meditation) in English; and a selection of poems from English, Hebrew, and Yiddish. The opening and closing lines, set in gray boxes, form the "frame" of each section and, when read together, are intended as blessings. The *kavanot* (meditations), which are in short paragraphs set in italic, are intended to stimulate spiritual focus on the content of the blessings and on the overall themes of the sections. The poems, which are written by various Jewish women poets, are unlike the other elements of this Amidah in that they provide a mixture of different voices. This variety is intended to encourage pray-ers to add their own voices to the conversation.

The new blessings, composed especially for this prayer, derive their language and imagery in large part from traditional sources, such as Bible and Hebrew liturgy. The English and Hebrew versions of the blessings are not exact equivalents. This is because they were not, strictly speaking, translated from each other. Rather, they were first composed in Hebrew, then in English, capturing the intended themes through the resources of each language.

May the words of this prayer touch and heal those who use them, and empower the silent to find voices of their own. MARCIA FALK

1. RE-CALLING OUR ANCESTORS, RE-MEMBERING OUR LIVES

נִזְכֹּר אֶת מָסֹרֶת הַדּוֹרוֹת
וְנִשְׁזֹר בָּהּ אֶת שָׂרִיגֵי חַיֵּינוּ.

Let us weave the branches of our lives
into the tradition.

Looking back can illumine; origins reveal meanings. Tradition—"to deliver, hand over"; masoret—*"to hand over," also perhaps "to tie." Tradition,* masoret, *is not just what we receive; it is the weaving of our own hands that we then hand over, the ties we make with past and future. Re-calling our past, we re-member our selves, making the branches part of the whole again.*

FROM MY MOTHER'S HOUSE

My mother's mother died
in the spring of her years,
and her daughter forgot her face.
Her portrait, engraved
on my grandfather's heart,
was erased from the world of images
when he died.

In the house, just her mirror remained,
sunk with age in its silver frame.
And I, the pale grandchild
who does not resemble her,
peer into it today as into a lake
that hides its treasures underwater.

Deep behind my face,
I see a young woman—
pink-cheeked, smiling,
a wig on her head—
threading a long-looped earring
through the tender flesh of her lobe.

Deep behind my face,
shines the bright gold of her eyes.
And the mirror passes on
the family lore:
She was very beautiful.

מִבֵּית אִמִּי

מֵתָה אִמָּהּ שֶׁל אִמִּי
בַּאֲבִיב יָמֶיהָ. וּבִתָּהּ
לֹא זָכְרָה אֶת פָּנֶיהָ. דְּיוֹקְנָהּ הֶחָרוּט
עַל לִבּוֹ שֶׁל סָבִי
נִמְחָה מֵעוֹלַם הַדְּמוּיוֹת
אַחֲרֵי מוֹתוֹ.

רַק הָרְאִי שֶׁלָּהּ נִשְׁתַּיֵּר בַּבַּיִת.
הֶעֱמִיק מֵרֹב שָׁנִים בְּמִשְׁבֶּצֶת הַכֶּסֶף.
וַאֲנִי, נֶכְדָתָהּ הַחִוֶּרֶת. שֶׁאֵינֶנִּי דּוֹמָה לָהּ,
מַבִּיטָה הַיּוֹם אֶל תּוֹכוֹ כְּאֶל תּוֹךְ
אֲגַם הַטּוֹמֵן אוֹצְרוֹתָיו
מִתַּחַת לַמַּיִם.

עָמֹק מְאֹד, מֵאֲחוֹרֵי פָּנַי,
אֲנִי רוֹאָה אִשָּׁה צְעִירָה
וְרֻדַּת לְחָיַיִם מְחַיֶּכֶת.
וּפֵאָה נָכְרִית לְרֹאשָׁהּ.
הִיא עוֹנֶדֶת
עָגִיל מָאֳרָךְ אֶל תְּנוּךְ אָזְנָהּ. מַשְׁחִילַתְהוּ
בְּנֶקֶב זָעִיר בַּבָּשָׂר הֶעָנֹג
שֶׁל הָאֹזֶן.

עָמֹק מְאֹד, מֵאֲחוֹרֵי פָּנַי, קוֹרֶנֶת
זְהוּבִית בְּהִירָה שֶׁל עֵינֶיהָ.
וְהָרְאִי מַמְשִׁיךְ אֶת מָסֹרֶת
הַמִּשְׁפָּחָה:
שֶׁהִיא הָיְתָה יָפָה מְאֹד.

EATING AN APPLE

The little paring knife
with the cool, round, ivory handle
took pride in being
in my grandpa's Sabbath hand
when
he would peel an apple,
and slowly lift to his lips
the thin, ripe, fragrant slices,
and say the blessing over the fruit of the tree.

He was a fine and pious grandpa, and behaved
as a pious grandpa should.

I'm a kid with an apple in my hand.
I dig my teeth in, lustily.

אַ ייִנגלינג מיט אַן עפּל אין האַנט

דאָס קליין מעסערל מיטן ווייסן,
קילן, קײַלעכדיקן העלפֿאַנטביין הענטל
האָט זיך געגרויסט
אין מײַן זיידנס שבתדיקער האַנט
בשעת
ער האָט אַן עפּל געשיילט
און דינינקע רייף־שמעקעדיקע ריפּטעלעך
פֿאַמעלעכקע צום מויל געטראָגן
און זײַנע ליפּן האָבן אַ ברכה געמאַכט
אויף פּרי פֿון בוים.

ער איז געווען אַן איידעלער זיידע־ייִד
און האָט געטאָן
ווי אַן איידעלער זיידע־ייִד.

איך בין
אַ ייִנגלינג מיט אַן עפּל אין האַנט.
איך בייס די צײַן אַרײַן
פֿאַרשייט.

איך בין פרוי / I AM WOMAN

איך בין די עקזולטירטע רחל וועמעס ליבע האָט באַלויכטן
דעם וועג פון די רבי עקיבאס.

I am the exalted Rachel
whose love lit the way for Rabbi Akiba.

איך בין דאָס קליינע, שעמעוודיקע דאָרף־מיידל וואָס איז
צווישן הויכע טאָפּאָלן געוואָקסן און זיך גערויטלט ביים
"גוט מאָרגן" פון ברודערס מלמד.

I am the small, bashful village girl
who grew up among the tall poplars
and blushed at the "good morning" of her brother's tutor.

איך בין דאָס פרומע מיידל וואָס האָט זיך געבלייכט ביי
דער מאַמעס ציטערדיקע פינגער אויף די אויגן אַנטקעגן די
בענטשליכט.

I am the pious girl
who paled as her mother raised her hands to her eyes
for the blessing over the Sabbath candles.

איך בין דאָס געהאָרכזאַם כלה־מיידל וואָס האָט הכנעהדיק
דאָס קעפּל אונטערגעטראָגן צום שער ערב הופה.

I am the obedient bride
who humbly bent her head beneath the shears
the night before the wedding.

איך בין די אשת־חיל וואָס האָט זיך אונטערגענומען געבערן
און שפּייזן פאַר אַביסעלע צוגעזאָגט גן עדן־ליכט.

I am the woman of valor
who bore and fed children
to earn herself a little place in paradise.

איך בין די אויסגעאיידלטע בת תלמיד חכם וואָס האָט מיט איר אָפּגעהיט לייב אַ שטאָט אַ יידישע מציל געווען און נאָכדעם מיט אייגענע הענט זיך אונטערגעצונדן.

I am the rabbi's daughter
who offered her chaste body to save a Jewish town
and afterwards set fire to herself.

איך בין די מאַמע וואָס האָט אונטער ענויים קשים ביז אין דער דאָר אַריין, בנים מגדל געווען צו מעשים טובים.

I am the mother
who, in great hardship,
raised sons to be righteous men.

איך בין די חסידישע טאָכטער וואָס האָט מיטן טאַטנס התלהבות געטראָגן דאָס געשוירן קעפּל אין פאָלק אַריין.

I am the Hasid's daughter,
infused with her father's fervor,
who went out defiant, with her hair cropped,
to educate the people.

איך בין די צוימען־ברעכערן וואָס האָט ״ברויט און פרייהייט״ נעטיילט און די ליבע באַפרייט פון אונטער חופּה־שטאַנגען.

I am the barrier-breaker
who freed love from the wedding canopy.

איך בין דאָס פאַרצערטלט מיידל וואָס האָט זיך הינטערן אַקער געשטעלט גרויען מדבר צו גרין לעבן באַצווינגען.

I am the pampered girl
who set herself behind a plow
to force the gray desert into green life.

איך בין דאָס מיידל וואָס האָט אירע ווייסע הענט באַפּעלן ציגל און שטיינער צו טראָגן צום אויפקום פון לעבן באַנייטן.

איך בין די וועמעס פינגער שטייפן אַרום רידל אין לויער פון טריט פון פאַרוויסטער.

I am the one whose fingers
tightened around the hoe,
on guard for the steps of the enemy.

איך בין די וואָס טראָגט פאַרעקשנט אַרום אַן אלף־בית אַ מאָדנעם און רוים אים אין קינדערשע אויערלעך איין.

I am the one who stubbornly
carries around a strange alphabet
to implant in children's ears.

איך בין אָט די אַלע און נאָך אַ סך, אַ סך ניט דערמאָנטע.

I am all these and many more.

און אומעטום,
און אַלעמאָל
בין איך
פרוי.

And everywhere, always, I am woman.

נִזְכֹּר אֶת מָסֹרֶת הַדּוֹרוֹת
וְנִשְׁזוֹר בָּהּ אֶת שָׂרִיגֵי חַיֵּינוּ

Let us weave the branches of our lives
into the tradition.

נְבָרֵךְ אֶת עֵין הַחַיִּים
וְכֹה נִתְבָּרֵךְ.

As we bless the source of life
so we are blessed.

2. SUSTAINING LIFE, EMBRACING DEATH

נְבָרֵךְ אֶת הַמַּעְיָן
עֲדֵי־עַד מְפַכֶּה —
מַעְגַּל הַחַיִּים
הַמֵּמִית וּמְחַיֶּה.

Let us bless the well
eternally giving—
the circle of life
ever-living, ever-dying.

To celebrate life is to acknowledge the ongoing dying, and ultimately to embrace death. For although all life travels toward its death, death is not a destination: it too is a journey to beginnings: all death leads to life again. From peelings to mulch to new potatoes, the world is forever renewed—

In everything, there is at least an eighth
of death. It doesn't weigh much.
With what hidden, peaceful charm
we carry it everywhere we go.
In sweet awakenings,
in our travels,
in our love talk,
when we are unaware,
forgotten in all the corners of our being—
always with us.
And never heavy.

. . .

בְּכָל דָּבָר יֵשׁ לְפָחוֹת שְׁמִינִית
שֶׁל מָ֫וֶת. מִשְׁקָלוֹ אֵינוֹ גָּדוֹל.
בְּאֵיזֶה חֵן טָמִיר וְשַׁאֲנָן
נִשָּׂא אוֹתוֹ אֶל כָּל אֲשֶׁר נֵלֵךְ.
בִּיקִיצוֹת יָפוֹת, בְּטִיּוּלִים,
בְּשִׂ֫יחַ אוֹהֲבִים, בְּהֶסַּח־דַּ֫עַת
נִשְׁכָּח בְּיַרְכְּתֵי הֲוָיָתֵ֫נוּ
תָּמִיד אִתָּ֫נוּ. וְאֵינוֹ מַכְבִּיד.

THE INVISIBLE CARMEL

When I die
to become another essence,
the invisible Mount Carmel—
which is all mine, all
the quintessence of joy,
whose needles, cones, flowers, and clouds
are carved into my flesh—
will part from the visible Carmel
with its boulevard of pinetrees
descending to the sea.

Does the pleasure of a red sunset
come from the mortal element in me?
And the pleasure of earth's perfumes,
and the moment when the sea bursts into spray,
and the moment of return
to the stern gaze of Jerusalem's sky,
to the Supreme One—
is all this from the mortal element?

הכרמל האי־נראה

כַּאֲשֶׁר אָמוּת
לַעֲבֹר לְמַהוּת אַחֶרֶת —
יִפָּרֵד הַכַּרְמֶל הָאִי־נִרְאֶה
שֶׁהוּא כֻּלּוֹ שֶׁלִּי,
כֻּלּוֹ תַּמְצִית הָאֹשֶׁר,
שֶׁמְּחָטָיו, אִצְטְרֻבָּלָיו, פְּרָחָיו וַעֲנָנָיו
חֲקוּקִים בִּבְשָׂרִי —
מִן הַכַּרְמֶל הַנִּרְאֶה
עִם שְׂדֵרַת הָאֳרָנִים שֶׁיּוֹרֶדֶת לַיָּם.

הַאִם תַּעֲנוּג הַשְּׁקִיעָה הָאֲדֻמָּה
הוּא מִיסוֹד הַתְּמוּתָה שֶׁבִּי?
וְתַעֲנוּג הַבְּשָׂמִים
וְרֶגַע עַרְפִלֵּי הַמַּיִם
וְרֶגַע הַשִּׁיבָה
לַמַּבָּט הַתַּקִּיף שֶׁל שְׁמֵי יְרוּשָׁלַיִם,
לָעֶלְיוֹן עַל הַכֹּל —
הַאִם מִיסוֹד הַתְּמוּתָה הוּא?

LEAVES

Leaves don't fall. They descend.
Longing for earth, they come winging.
In their time, they'll come again,
For leaves don't fall. They descend.
On the branches, they will be again.
Green and fragrant, cradle-swinging,
For leaves don't fall. They descend.
Longing for earth, they come winging.

בלעטער

בלעטער פאַלן ניט. זיי נידערן.
ערד־פאַרבענקטע זיי קומען פליגלדיק.
אין זייער צײַט זיי וועלן ווידער ווידערן,
ווײַל בלעטער פאַלן ניט. זיי נידערן.
זיי וועלן ווידער מיט די צווײַגן גלידערן
גרין און שמעקעדיק און וויגלדיק
ווײַל בלעטער פאַלן ניט. זיי נידערן.
ערד־פאַרבענקטע זיי קומען פליגלדיק.

DIALOGUES

The waving blue arms of the elm
and the agitated answer of the green fig,

the fat globes of yellow sugarmum
where bees suck love,

and you, in the morning's shade,
sipping hot coffee—

the darkbrown taste of the beans
and the milky froth—

say:

Indulge: the world
is abundant,
and ceaselessly dying—

This loving, dying world
to which we are given,
out of which we have come—

O body of the world,
eat with joy
the body of the world!

Let us bless the well eternally giving— the circle of life ever-dying, ever-living.	נְבָרֵךְ אֶת הַמַּעְיָן עֲדֵי־עַד מְפַכֶּה — מַעְגַּל הַחַיִּים הַמֵּמִית וּמְחַיֶּה.
As we bless the wellspring of life, so we are blessed.	נְבָרֵךְ אֶת עֵין הַחַיִּים וְכֹה נִתְבָּרֵךְ.

3. HALLOWING OUR NAMINGS

Let us sing the soul in every name and the names of every soul.	נָשִׁיר לְנִשְׁמַת כָּל שֵׁם וּלְשֵׁם כָּל נְשָׁמָה.

EACH OF US HAS A NAME

Each of us has a name
given by God
and given by our parents
Each of us has a name
given by our stature and our smile
and given by what we wear
Each of us has a name
given by the mountains
and given by our walls
Each of us has a name
given by the stars
and given by our neighbors
Each of us has a name
given by our sins
and given by our longing
Each of us has a name
given by our enemies
and given by our love
Each of us has a name
given by our celebrations
and given by our work
Each of us has a name
given by the seasons
and given by our blindness

Each of us has a name
given by the sea
and given by
our death.

Naming—our most human act. With words and images, we name the world, name toward the divine. As tradition repeatedly tells us, the more we recount and name, the more we increase the presence of the holy in the world. The more names with which we point toward divinity, the closer we approach the inclusive vision of the One.

נָשִׁיר לְנִשְׁמַת כָּל שֵׁם
וּלְשֵׁם כָּל נְשָׁמָה.

Let us sing the soul in every name
and the names of every soul.

נְבָרֵךְ אֶת עֵין הַחַיִּים
וְכֹה נִתְבָּרֵךְ.

As we bless the source of life
so we are blessed.

4. HALLOWING THE SABBATH

נְקַדֵּשׁ אֶת יוֹם הַשַּׁבָּת
זֵכֶר לְמַעֲשֵׂה בְרֵאשִׁית.

Let us hallow the Sabbath day
in remembrance of creation.

Sabbath: there is the part that we make happen, through our acts of will—

WILL

Three generations back
my family had only

to light a candle
and the world parted.

Today, Friday afternoon,
I disconnect clocks and phones.

When night fills my house
with passages,

I begin saving
my life.

הדליקו נר	**LIGHT A CANDLE**
הַדְלִיקוּ נֵר	Light a candle,
שְׁתוּ יַיִן.	drink wine.
הַשַּׁבָּת קָטְפָה בַּלָּאט	Softly the Sabbath has plucked
אֶת הַשֶּׁמֶשׁ הַשּׁוֹקַעַת.	the sinking sun.
הַשַּׁבָּת יוֹרֶדֶת לְאַט	Slowly the Sabbath descends,
וּבְיָדָהּ שׁוֹשַׁנַּת הָרְקִיעִים.	the rose of heaven in her hand.
אֵיךְ תִּשְׁתֹּל הַשַּׁבָּת	How can the Sabbath
פֶּרַח עָצוּם וּמֵאִיר	plant a huge and shining flower
בְּלֵב צַר וְעִוֵּר?	in a blind and narrow heart?
אֵיךְ תִּשְׁתֹּל הַשַּׁבָּת	How can the Sabbath
אֶת צִיץ הַמַּלְאָכִים	plant the bud of angels
בְּלֵב בָּשָׂר מְשֻׁגָּע וְהוֹלֵל?	in a heart of raving flesh?
הֲתִצְמַח שׁוֹשַׁנַּת הָאַלְמָוֶת	Can the rose of eternity grow
בְּדוֹר שֶׁל עֲבָדִים	among the slaves
לַהֶרֶס,	of destruction,
בְּדוֹר שֶׁל עֲבָדִים	among the slaves
לַמָּוֶת?!	of death?
הַדְלִיקוּ נֵר!	Light a candle!
שְׁתוּ יַיִן!	Drink wine!
הַשַּׁבָּת יוֹרֶדֶת בַּלָּאט	Slowly the Sabbath descends
וּבְיָדָהּ הַפֶּרַח,	and in her hand
וּבְיָדָהּ	the flower,
הַשֶּׁמֶשׁ הַשּׁוֹקַעַת . . .	and in her hand
	the sinking sun.

And then—

SATURDAY MORNING, EARLY MAY

In the green and yellow grass of the broad field
fringed by greening trees,
leaves flapping,
birds talking and flapping,
a young girl disappears.
She lies down in her bright shirt
into the soft green grass
and disappears.

Later, the girl rises from her bed in the grass
and lifts her head among the white-topped stalks of clover.
She rises and walks off,
wading down into the field,
which waves around her like a lake—
so that soon she imagines she is sailing on a summer lake,
her body light as a sail in the fresh cold breeze.

All this is seen by the woman who sits on the roof.
She sits on the sun-warmed roof
and watches the tree-ringed field rock and sway
around the bobbing head of a girl wading through the
weeds.

This is the picture the woman sees:
field, girl, bluejay, trees.
No matter what happens outside of this,
the girl will always be part of this.

Then, for a tiny instant,
the woman is weightless in the galaxy
which floats around her, blue and indifferent
and fierce as a winter sea.

This is the miracle, which we can only receive: when it happens, releasing us from time, all of creation is one, and we are one with it. Though momentary, it is a recollection of our earliest origins, and a glimpse of time to come.

נְקַדֵּשׁ אֶת יוֹם הַשַּׁבָּת
זֵֽכֶר לְמַעֲשֵׂה בְרֵאשִׁית.

Let us hallow the Sabbath day
in remembrance of creation.

נְבָרֵךְ אֶת עֵין הַחַיִּים
וְכֹה נִתְבָּרֵךְ.

As we bless the source of life
so we are blessed.

5. RESTORING TO SHEḤINAH HER PLACE

נַחֲזִיר מָקוֹם לַשְּׁכִינָה
וְאֶת הַשְּׁכִינָה לְכָל מָקוֹם.

Let us restore to *Sheḥinah* her place
and infuse all places with her presence.

Sheḥinah—*a traditional feminine name for divinity—has long been the symbol of divinity in exile, divinity abandoned. Ironic, because the word itself means "indwelling." That* Sheḥinah *should have been portrayed as homeless when she was the very embodiment of home, is not only ironic—it is also symbolic. Many Jewish women identify with the image of* Sheḥinah, *and as we yearn for a return to our home, our rightful place in the tradition, we ask that all indwelling be honored—all place, all body, all matter that has been maligned, profaned, and abused, be hallowed once again.*

RECOVERY

The sky is soft as a grandmother's quilt, fleecy as sheep—
sheep as you imagine them to be, not as they are.

The leaves and grass are soft, too.
They seem to heal you with their green fingers,
their heady perfumes rising.

The wind will open its arms, the field will catch you in its lap,
they will rock you, rock you like a baby
as you dreamed it in your deepest longing,

not as it happens when you wish for it
but as it's told in an old old story,
a story you were born knowing and later forgot.

נַחֲזִיר מָקוֹם לַשְּׁכִינָה
וְאֶת הַשְּׁכִינָה לְכָל מָקוֹם.

Let us restore to *Sheḥinah* her place
and infuse all places with her presence.

נְבָרֵךְ אֶת עֵין הַחַיִּים
וְכֹה נִתְבָּרֵךְ.

As we bless the source of life
so we are blessed.

6. THE GIFT OF GRATITUDE

בְּפֶה מָלֵא שִׁירָה כַּיָּם
וּבְלָשׁוֹן רְווּיַת רִנָּה —

With mouths full of song as the sea
and tongues overflowing with joy—

Out of silence, in the opened space, the song of gratitude is born—

כְּפֶה מָלֵא שִׁירָה כַּיָּם
וּבְלָשׁוֹן רְווּיַת רִנָּה —
נְבָרֵךְ אֶת עֵין הַחַיִּים
וְכֹה נִתְבָּרֵךְ.

With mouths full of song as the sea
and tongues overflowing with joy—

We bless the source of life
and so we are blessed.

7. THE BLESSINGS OF PEACE

יְהִי שָׁלוֹם טוֹבָה וּבְרָכָה
חֵן וָחֶסֶד וְרַחֲמִים
בֵּינֵינוּ, בֵּין כָּל עֲדוֹת יִשְׂרָאֵל
וּבֵין כָּל יוֹשְׁבֵי תֵּבֵל.

May the blessings of peace enfold and infuse,
embrace and intertwine
all of Israel and all the world.

For millennia, the flood has been a symbol of world destruction; yet today it is the fire we must fear. So water may be redeemed as a saving image, becoming again the water of redemption. We are told that our bodies are composed, mostly, of water—water, and breath. It is time to reclaim the power of our bodies—the power of our physical acts—and save the fragile body of the world. But to do that, we must first imagine the possibility, and give voice to the vision of a world at peace.

. . . . . .

הַגֶּשֶׁם הָרִאשׁוֹן	The first rain—
אַלְפֵי רְבָבָה רַעֲנַנּוּת	a plethora of freshness
בְּלִי אוֹת שֶׁל קַיִן.	with no sign of Cain.
וְהַדְּוַי לֹא יִלְחַשׁ עוֹד	And agony will no longer
לְנַפְשִׁי	whisper to my soul:
אֲנִי הַמֶּלֶךְ	I am the king.
לֹא יַגִּיד עוֹד	No longer will it say:
אֲנִי הַשַּׁלִּיט.	I am the ruler.
כָּל טִפָּה וְטִפָּה	Each and every drop
הִיא זִקָּה	is a link
בֵּינִי וּבֵין הַדְּבָרִים	between me and things,
זִקָּה	a link
בֵּינִי וּבֵין הָעוֹלָם.	between me and the world.
וְכַאֲשֶׁר הַלַּיְלָה	And when night
מַעֲלֶה אֶת הַתְּהוֹם	conjures up the abyss,
הַתְּהוֹם מַעֲלֶה	the abyss conjures up
שָׂדוֹת וְגַנִּים.	fields and gardens.

נִשְׁאַל מֵעֵין הַשָּׁלוֹם:
יִזַּל כַּטַּל
יַעֲרֹף כַּמָּטָר הַשָּׁלוֹם.
וְנַקְדִּישׁ חַיֵּינוּ לְהַגְשָׁמָתוֹ
עַד שֶׁתִּמְלָא הָאָרֶץ בּוֹ
כַּמַּיִם לַיָּם מְכַסִּים.

Eternal wellspring of peace—
May we be drenched with the longing for peace
that we may give ourselves over to peace
until the earth overflows with peace
as living waters overflow the seas.

יְהִי שָׁלוֹם טוֹבָה וּבְרָכָה
חֵן וָחֶסֶד וְרַחֲמִים
בֵּינֵינוּ, בֵּין כָּל עֲדוֹת יִשְׂרָאֵל
וּבֵין כָּל יוֹשְׁבֵי תֵבֵל.

May the blessings of peace enfold and infuse,
embrace and intertwine
all of Israel and all the world.

נְבָרֵךְ אֶת עֵין הַחַיִּים
וְכֹה נִתְבָּרֵךְ.

As we bless the source of life
so we are blessed.

*   *

AMIDAH MEDITATIONS

These meditations (pages 179 to 183) are alternatives to the Shabbat Amidah. Traditionally recited thrice daily, the Amidah originally served as a time for meditation. That path is inaccessible to many of us. These meditations are intended to restore it. They can be self-guided or leader-directed. Leaders might guide a whole congregation or groups as small as two or three. Leadership can be rotated.

In meditating with a leader/guide, participants are led by the guide's voice. If the leader moves too quickly for you, move at your own pace, allowing your mind to carry you until you are again in step with the leader. In meditating without a leader/guide, select a meditation and read the instructions. Then close your eyes and sit comfortably, with both feet on the ground, hands resting loosely in your lap. Take a few deep breaths, then begin the meditation. Be careful not to let your thoughts wander—if they do, bring them back by taking a few deep breaths. Proceed at your own pace. Do not hurry. When you have completed one meditation, feel free to begin another.

A single meditation, or up to three, might serve as the Amidah.

1. AVOT

Think about the people to whom you answer. . . . Who is your inner "board of directors"? . . . Who is it you are serving in your life? . . . Who are your Abrahams, Isaacs, Jacobs, your Sarahs, Rebekahs, Rachels and Leahs? . . . Don't struggle with the voices or engage them in any way. . . . Simply acknowledge them. . . . Invite them into your Shabbat. . . . Feel at one with them.

2. GEVUROT

Think of a part of your present life—a personality, relationship, or situation—that feels stagnant to you. . . . Something isn't right. It isn't growing. There is a lifeless quality to it. . . . Imagine how you might enliven that part of your life. What things might you do to bring that change about? . . . Now think of a part of your life you have enlivened, either recently or over the years. . . . Allow yourself to feel gratitude and joy for that.

3. KEDUSHAT HASHEM

Slowly recite this chant to yourself: *Atah kadosh, shimeḥa kadosh, ve'anu kedoshim.* Try to feel the rhythm of this chant. If it is comfortable for you, stand as you chant, bow to the right and to the left, then raise your hands and look up. The literal meaning of this chant is: "You are holy, your name is holy, and we are holy beings." As you recite this chant, allow yourself to feel the holiness of all life, and the holy cycles of life.

4. KEDUSHAT HAYOM

Remember a moment in your life when you felt a sense of perfection. . . . Try to dwell on images of that moment until they are completely in focus: the visual image, the sounds, the physical sensations, the emotions. Do not rush this. . . . Try to recapture that sense of perfection and think, "this is my Shabbat, this is my Shabbat."

5. AVODAH

Imagine a long table, around which is gathered your ideal community. Focus on the different members of that ideal community. Feel the sense of awe and thanksgiving at such a miracle. Immerse yourself in those feelings of joy. Take that sense of joy and refocus it on the community of Israel, regathered in our homeland, and the joy that brings you. Allow yourself to take in the miracle of that ingathering.

6. HODA'AH

Recall a recent event in your life for which you would like to offer thanks. Focus on that one event for a moment. Allow your mind to associate freely. Remember other events in your life that have evoked in you a sense of thanksgiving. Feel yourself immersed in a sea of blessings that have occurred in your life, and for which you now offer thanks.

7. BIRKAT HASHALOM

(a) Take a few deep breaths. Breathe in. Then breathe out the sound "Sha," then breathe in the sound "lom." Keep your breathing slow and even. Feel the sense of inner peace that this breathing echoes.

(b) Remember a time in your life when someone acted as a peace-maker between you and another person. Feel what a powerful role that was. Remember a different time when you acted as a peacemaker for others. Feel the sense of satisfaction that experience brought you. Now imagine other ways in your life that you might act as a peace-maker. Feel the sense of power and gratitude that those images bring.

8. SHIVITI MEDITATION

The *Shiviti* is a spiritual tool. It provides a visual focus for efforts to sense the divine presence. Facing that presence through the *Shiviti* design, feeling surrounded by the divine, embracing the divine within ourselves leads to awareness of the fullness of God—and to the godliness which fills us. The *Shiviti* meditation can yield new insight—a sense of harmony and balance. It can give us a sense of our place in the order of things. It can provide fresh perspective, clarity, and energy. The *Shiviti* design is on page 97. The first-time user can begin by exploring the *Shiviti*—responding to its overall shape, reading its words, contemplating their meanings. More focused meditations on the *Shiviti* appear below.

(a) Let the fullness of this *Shiviti* flow over you. . . . Slowly begin to focus on one of the psalm verses on the *Shiviti* page. Breathe in and out slowly and steadily. . . . Now close your eyes. Visualize the *yud hey vav hey*. . . . Slowly chant to yourself the words of your verse. Let all extraneous thoughts flow away from you. Allow yourself to feel the presence of God.

(b) Let the fullness of this *Shiviti* flow over you. Breathe steadily. Begin to focus on the *yud hey vav hey.* Close your eyes. Visualize the יהוה. . . . See it vertically, with the *yud* on top. Reach for the holiness it embodies. . . . Now begin to focus on the *yud.* Visualize your head as a *yud.* . . . Focus on the *hey.* Visualize your shoulders as a *hey.* . . . Focus on the *vav.* Visualize your trunk as a *vav.* . . . Focus on the final *hey.* Now visualize your legs as a *hey.* . . . Breathe slowly. Feel the godliness rise and fall within you, with each breath. Focus on your sense of oneness, of unity, with the divine.

(c) Let the fullness of this *Shiviti* flow over you. Breathe steadily. Begin to focus on the יהוה. . . . Close your eyes. As you focus on the *yud,* empty your breath slowly, for a count of four. . . . As you focus on the *hey,* breathe in slowly for a count of four, softly making the sound of *hey.* . . . As you focus on the *vav,* hold your breath for a count of four. . . . As you focus on the final *hey,* begin to breathe out for a count of four, softly making the sound of *hey.* . . . Repeat this breathing exercise several times, holding each point for a count of four. Feel godliness flowing in and out of you, and flowing all around you. Feel the links to all other breathing vessels of God. . . . Now feel the godliness in all the other vessels of the divine, the divine bridges through all creation, the bridges that make us one.

*   *

A SHORT AMIDAH

They say we're supposed to be in a palace.
So we bow and take certain steps
as the prescribed supplication
drops from our lips.
But what do we really know
of castles and kings?
My kitchen faucet constantly leaks
and the kids' faces
usually need cleaning.
If a door opened to a real palace,
I'd probably forget
and carry in a load of groceries.

No, the door we stand in front of
when the Amidah begins is silence.
And when we open it
and step through,
we arrive in our hearts.
Mine's not a fancy place,
no jewels, no throne,
certainly not fit for a king.
But in that small chamber,
for just a few moments on Sabbath,
God and I can roll up our sleeves,
put some schnapps out on the table,
sit down together, and finally talk.
That's palace enough for me.

Syd Lieberman

*   *

READINGS

SHABBAT THEMES

Song of the Sabbath

I quarreled with kings till the Sabbath,
I fought with the six kings
of the six days of the week.

Sunday they took away my sleep.
Monday they scattered my salt.
And on the third day, my God,
they threw out my bread: whips flashed
across my face. The fourth day
they caught my dove, my flying dove,
and slaughtered it.
It was like that till Friday morning.

This is my whole week,
the dove's flight dying.

At nightfall Friday
I lit four candles,
and the queen of the Sabbath came to me.
Her face lit up the whole world,
and made it all a Sabbath.
My scattered salt
shone in its little bowl,
and my dove, my flying dove,
clapped its wings together,
and licked its throat.
The Sabbath queen blessed my candles,
and they burned with a pure, clean flame.
The light put out the days of the week
and my quarreling with the six kings. כ

The greenness of the mountains
is the greenness of the Sabbath.
The silver of the lake
is the silver of the Sabbath.
The singing of the wind
is the singing of the Sabbath.

And my heart's song
is an eternal Sabbath.

Kadia Molodowsky (translated from Yiddish)

Wellfleet Sabbath

The hawk eye of the sun slowly shuts.
The breast of the bay is softly feathered
dove grey. The sky is barred like the sand
when the tide trickles out.

The great doors of the Sabbath are swinging
open over the ocean, loosing the moon
floating up slow   distorted   vast, a copper
balloon just sailing free.

The wind slides over the waves, patting
them with its giant hand, and the sea
stretches its muscles in the deep,
purrs and rolls over.

The sweet beeswax candles flicker
and sigh, standing between the phlox
and the roast chicken. The wine shines
its red lantern of joy.

Here on this piney sandspit, the Shekhinah
comes on the short strong wings of the seaside
sparrow raising her song and bringing
down the fresh clean night.

Marge Piercy

We know what to do with space but do not know what to do about time, except to make it subservient to space, or to while it away, to *kill time.* However, *time is life,* and to kill time is to murder. Most of us seem to labor for the sake of things of space. As a result we suffer from a deeply rooted dread of time and stand aghast when compelled to look into its face. Shrinking from facing time, we escape for shelter to things of space.

Most of us do not live in time but run away from it; we do not see its face, but its make-up. The past is either forgotten or preserved as a cliché, and the present moment is either bartered for a silly trinket or beclouded by false anticipations. The present moment is a zero, and so is the next moment, and a vast stretch of life turns out to be a series of zeros, with no real number in front.

Blind to the marvel of the present moment, we live with memories of moments missed, in anxiety about an emptiness that lies ahead. We are unprepared when the problem strikes us in unmitigated form.

Time is our most important frontier, the advance region of significant being, a region where our true freedom lies. Space divides us, time unites us. We wage wars over things of space; the treasures of time lie open to every one of us.

Time has independent ultimate significance; it is of more majesty and more evocative of awe than even a sky studded with stars. Gliding gently in the most ancient of all splendors, ↩

it tells so much more than space can say in its broken language of things, playing symphonies upon the instruments of isolated beings, unlocking the earth and making it happen. Time is the process of creation, and things of space are results of creation. When looking at space we see the products of creation; when intuiting time we hear the process of creation. Things of space exhibit a deceptive independence. They show off a veneer of limited permanence. Things created conceal the Creator. It is the dimension of time wherein we meet God, wherein we become aware that every instant is an act of creation, a Beginning, opening up new roads for ultimate realizations. *Time is the presence of God in the world of space,* and it is within time that we are able to sense the unity of all beings.

Abraham Joshua Heschel

The Sabbath expresses for modern Jews, as it did for their ancestors, the thought that the world is so constituted that we can achieve salvation if, by adhering to valid ideals, we put ourselves in contact with the creative forces that shape life and make it worth living. Since we identify God with that aspect of reality which gives to life its supreme value or holiness, this is but another way of saying in more traditional language that the Sabbath expresses for us the faith that humanity can achieve salvation by cleaving to God, the Source of salvation.

But the Sabbath is not only a symbol of the salvation to be achieved by communion with God. It is itself an instrument that we may employ to advantage in our pursuit of salvation. We need perhaps more than ever before to terminate each week with a day that shall stimulate our thirst for salvation and keep us faithful to the ideals that lead to its attainment. Otherwise our mere pre-occupation with the business of "making a living," that is, of securing the conditions indispensable to life, tends to absorb all our attention, and life ↩

itself becomes empty and meaningless. We work to keep alive that we may work to keep alive, until our powers are spent in this weary treadmill, and death brings surcease of labor. If life is to be lived zestfully, and to employ all those human faculties the full exercise of which calls forth true joy in being alive, we dare not permit life to sink to such a level of mere preoccupation with the problem of survival. The Sabbath, with its insistence upon interrupting the routine of our daily business and concerning ourselves with spiritual values, helps to save us from such a fate.

Mordecai M. Kaplan (adapted)

NATURE THEMES

I look up to the sky and the stars,
And down to the earth and the things that creep there,
And I consider in my heart how their creation
Was planned with wisdom in every detail.
See the heavens above like a tent,
Constructed with loops and hooks,
And the moon with its stars, like a shepherdess
Sending her sheep into the reeds;
The moon itself among the clouds,
Like a ship sailing under its banners;
The clouds like a girl in her garden
Moving, and watering the myrtle-trees;
The dew-mist—a woman shaking
Drops from her hair to the ground.
The inhabitants turn, like animals, to rest,
(Their palaces are their stables);
And all fleeing from the fear of death, ↩

Like a dove pursued by the falcon.
And these are compared at the end to a plate
Which is smashed into innumerable shards.

Shmuel Hanagid (translated from Hebrew)

Where We Can Find God

Where will I find God
Whose glory fills the universe?

I find God
Wherever the farmer ploughs a furrow through the hard soil,
Wherever the quarryman pounds the stone to gravel,
Wherever one earns her bread by the sweat of her brow,
In the company of the friendless, the afflicted, the lowly, the lost,
There God abides in sun and shower.

I find God
Wherever the mind is free to follow its own bent,
Wherever words come out from the depth of truth,
Wherever tireless striving stretches its arms toward perfection,
Wherever people struggle for freedom and right,
Wherever the scientist toils to unbare the secrets of nature,
Wherever the poet strings pearls of beauty in lyric lines,
Wherever glorious deeds are done.

I find God
In the merry shouts of children at play,
In the lullaby the mother sings, rocking her baby to sleep,
In the slumber that falls on the infant's eyelids,
And in the smile that plays on his sleeping lips.

I find God
When the dawn comes with her golden cornucopia,

Or when evening falls, bringing peace and rest from the
Western ocean of rest.
God is in the joy that streams from heaven with the morning
light,
In the current of life that courses day and night through my
sinews and through all nature,
In the life that throbs exultant in the dust of the earth and
through the blades of grass innumerable,
And that flows, in a multitude of tempestuous waves,
through the leaves and flowers.

I find God
In the wealth of those passing delights that live but for a
moment,
In the pulsebeat of a life that comes from eternity and dances
in my own blood,
In birth that keeps renewing the generations,
And in death that keeps knocking on the doors of life.

Rabindranath Tagore (translated and adapted)

God The Life of Nature

Our ancestors acclaimed the God
Whose handiwork they read
In the mysterious heavens above,
And in the varied scene of earth below,
In the orderly march of days and nights,
Of seasons and years,
And in the checkered fate of humankind.

Night reveals the limitless caverns of space,
Hidden by the light of day,
And unfolds horizonless vistas
Far beyond imagination's ken.
The mind is staggered,
Yet soon regains its poise,

And peering through the boundless dark,
Orients itself anew
By the light of distant suns
Shrunk to glittering sparks.
The soul is faint,
Yet soon revives,
And learns to spell once more the name of God
Across the newly visioned firmament.

  Lift your eyes, look up;
  Who made these stars?

God is the oneness
That spans the fathomless deeps of space
And the measureless eons of time,
Binding them together in deed,
As we do in thought.

God is the sameness
In the elemental substance of stars and planets,
Of this our earthly abode
And of all that it holds.

God is the unity
Of all that is,
The uniformity of all that moves,
The rhythm of all things
And the nature of their interaction.

God is the mystery of life,
Enkindling inert matter
With inner drive and purpose.

God is the creative flame
That transfigures lifeless substance,
Leaping into ever higher realms of being,
Brightening into the radiant glow of feeling,
Till it turns into the white fire of thought.

And though no sign of living things
Breaks the eternal silence of the spheres,
We cannot deem this earth,
This tiny speck in the infinitude,
Alone instinct with God.

By that token
Which unites the worlds in bonds of matter
Are all the worlds bound
In the bond of Life.

God is in the faith
By which we overcome
The fear of loneliness, of helplessness,
Of failure and of death.

God is in the hope
Which, like a shaft of light,
Cleaves the dark abysms
Of sin, of suffering, and of despair.

God is in the love
Which creates, protects, forgives.

It is God's spirit
That broods upon the chaos we have wrought,
Disturbing its static wrongs,
And stirring into life the formless beginnings
Of the new and better world.

Mordecai M. Kaplan (adapted)

In Praise

GENESIS 1, 2

Hail the hand that scattered space with stars,
Wrapped whirling world in bright blue blanket, air,
Made worlds within worlds, elements in earth, כ

Souls within skins, every one a teeming universe,
Every tree a system of semantics, and pushed
Beyond probability to place consciousness
On this cooling crust of burning rock.

Oh praise that hand, mind, heart, soul, power or force
That so inclosed, separated, limited planets, trees, humans
Yet breaks all bounds and borders
To lavish on us light, love, life
This trembling glory.

Ruth Brin

Trees

To be a giant and keep quiet about it,
To stay in one's own place;
To stand for the constant presence of process
And always to seem the same;
To be steady as a rock and always trembling,
Having the hard appearance of death
With the soft, fluent nature of growth,
One's Being deceptively armored,
One's Becoming deceptively vulnerable;
To be so tough, and take the light so well,
Freely providing forbidden knowledge
Of so many things about heaven and earth
For which we should otherwise have no word—
Poems or people are rarely so lovely,
And even when they have great qualities
They tend to tell you rather than exemplify
What they believe themselves to be about,
While from the moving silence of trees,
Whether in storm or calm, in leaf and naked,
Night or day, we draw conclusions of our own, ⮐

Sustaining and unnoticed as our breath,
And perilous also—though there has never been
A critical tree—about the nature of things.

Howard Nemerov

The Peace of Wild Things

When despair for the world grows in me
and I wake in the night at the least sound
in fear of what my life and my children's lives may be,
I go and lie down where the wood drake
rests in his beauty on the water, and the great heron feeds.
I come into the peace of wild things
who do not tax their lives with forethought
of grief. I come into the presence of still water.
And I feel above me the day-blind stars
waiting with their light. For a time
I rest in the grace of the world, and am free.

Wendell Berry

EXODUS THEMES

During the last two thousand years, Jews have never wearied of referring to the Exodus. In the morning and evening prayers, in the thanksgiving benediction after each meal, and in the Kiddush inaugurating Shabbat and Festivals, Jews have thanked God for having delivered their ancestors from Egypt. And every year with the return of the Festival of Pesaḥ they have recounted to their children the story of that redemption. The main motive which has kept alive the memory of the Exodus during the last two thousand years has undoubtedly been the hope that, as God had wrought miracles for Israel in the past, had been gracious to them and had delivered them from bondage, so will God, when the time comes, once again ↩

manifest power on behalf of the Jewish people, free them from oppression and restore them to their land.

Changes, however, have taken place in human life which render that simple version of the Exodus and its meaning no longer adequate. Jews are still the victims of oppression. But they have entered into such intimate relationship with the life of the world about them that they can no longer envisage their own deliverance except as a phase of general human deliverance. If miracles are to be enacted as part of the future redemption, they cannot be conceived as similar to those which tradition associates with the Exodus. The new redemption to which Jews look forward involves the redemption of society in general from present ills. It implies the transformation of human nature and social institutions through the divine power of intelligence and goodwill. There can be no question that in the Torah the story of the Exodus has the connotation that to help the oppressed is an essential attribute of godhood.

Mordecai M. Kaplan (adapted)

I Shall Sing to the Lord a New Song

I, Miriam, stand at the sea
and turn
to face the desert
stretching endless and
still.
My eyes are dazzled
The sky brilliant blue
Sunburnt sands unyielding white.
My hands turn to dove wings.
My arms
reach
for the sky ↩

and I want to sing
the song rising inside me.

My mouth open
I stop.
Where are the words?
Where the melody?

In a moment of panic
My eyes go blind.
Can I take a step
Without knowing a
Destination?
Will I falter
Will I fall
Will the ground sink away from under me?

The song still unformed—
How can I sing?

To take the first step—
To sing a new song—
Is to close one's eyes
and dive
into unknown waters.
For a moment knowing nothing risking all—
But then to discover

The waters are friendly
The ground is firm.
And the song—
the song rises again.
Out of my mouth
come words lifting the wind.
And I hear
for the first
the song
that has been in my heart

silent
unknown
even to me.

Ruth H. Sohn

We All Stood Together

My brother and I were at Sinai
He kept a journal
of what he saw
of what he heard
of what it all meant to him

I wish I had such a record
of what happened to me there

It seems like every time I want to write
I can't
I'm always holding a baby
one of my own
or one for a friend
always holding a baby
so my hands are never free
to write things down

And then
as time passes
the particulars
the hard data
the who what when where why
slip away from me
and all I'm left with is
the feeling

But feelings are just sounds
the vowel barking of a mute ↩

My brother is so sure of what he heard
after all he's got a record of it
consonant after consonant after consonant

If we remembered it together
we could recreate holy time
sparks flying

Merle Feld

So pharaonic oppression, deliverance, Sinai, and Canaan are still with us, powerful memories shaping our perceptions of the political world. The "door of hope" is still open; things are not what they might be—even when what they might be isn't totally different from what they are. . . . We still believe, or many of us do, what the Exodus first taught, or what it has commonly been taken to teach, about the meaning and possibility of politics and about its proper form:

—first, that wherever you live, it is probably Egypt;

—second, that there is a better place, a world more attractive, a promised land;

—and third, that "the way to the land is through the wilderness." There is no way to get from here to there except by joining together and marching.

Michael Walzer

PEACE THEMES

Shalom is one of the many names by which God is known in Judaism. It is the name by which God will bless you if you dedicate yourselves to each other in accordance with the divine will. The name *Shalom* embraces everything that is calculated to render life happy, useful and holy. It denotes, in the first place, love—love that is binding and everlasting, love that does not fade with the flowers or pass with the sunshine. *Shalom* is the peace that is secured when we have done our share toward our companions, whenever we bring light into hearts that are dark with despair and cheer into souls overcast with gloom. No language possesses a word that so accurately describes the serenity of the soul which we experience whenever we have thus made God's presence real to men and women. By seeking to promote the happiness of your neighbor, by engaging in every effort to be of help to your companion and by emphasizing that aspect of life that we call holy, you will realize the full blessing of love and peace, the blessing of *Shalom.*

Mordecai M. Kaplan (adapted)

We Mothers

We mothers,
we gather seeds of desire
from oceanic night,
we are gatherers
of scattered goods,

We mothers,
pacing dreamily
with the constellations,
the floods
of past and future,
leave us alone
with our birth
like an island.

We mothers
who say to death:
blossom in our blood, ↩

We who impel sand to love and bring
a mirroring world to the stars—

We mothers,
who rock in the cradles
the shadowy memories
of creation's day—
the to and fro of each breath
is the melody of our love song.

We mothers
rock into the heart of the world
the melody of peace.

Nelly Sachs (translated)

An Appendix to the Vision of Peace

Don't stop after beating the swords
into ploughshares, don't stop! Go on beating
and make musical instruments out of them.

Whoever wants to make war again
will have to turn them into ploughshares first.

Yehuda Amichai (translated from Hebrew)

Wildpeace

Not that of a cease-fire,
let alone the vision
of the wolf and the lamb,
but rather
as in the heart after a surge of emotion:
to speak only about a great weariness.
I know that I know how
to kill: that's why I'm an adult.

And my son plays with a toy gun that knows
how to open and close its eyes and say Mama.
A peace
without the big noise of beating swords into plowshares,
without words, without
the heavy thud of the rubber stamp; I want it
gentle over us, like lazy white foam.
A little rest for the wounds—
who speaks of healing?
(And the orphans' outcry is passed from one generation
to the next, as in a relay race:
that baton never falls.)

I want it to come
like wildflowers,
suddenly, because the field
needs it: wildpeace

Yehuda Amichai (translated from Hebrew)

Strange is our situation here upon earth. Each of us comes for a short visit, not knowing why, yet sometimes seeming to divine a purpose. From the standpoint of daily life, however, there is one thing we do know: that we are here for the sake of each other, above all, for those upon whose smile and well-being our own happiness depends, and also for the countless unknown souls with whose fate we are connected by a bond of sympathy. Many times a day I realize how much my own outer and inner life is built upon the labors of others, both living and dead, and how earnestly I must exert myself in order to give in return as much as I have received and am still receiving.

Albert Einstein (adapted)

PRAYER

A Sense of Your Presence

Among our many appetites
There is a craving after God.

Among our many attributes
There is a talent for worshiping God.

Jews who wandered in deserts beneath the stars
Knew their hearts were hungry for God.

Jews who studied in candle-lit ghetto rooms
Thirsted longingly after God.

In tent or hut or slum
Jewish women prayed to God.

But we who are smothered with comfort
Sometimes forget to listen.

Help us, O God, to recognize our need,
To hear the yearning whisper of our hearts.

Help us to seek the silence of the desert
And the thoughtfulness of the house of study.

Bless us, like our ancestors in ancient days
With that most precious gift: a sense of Your presence.

Brush us with the wind of the wings of Your being.
Fill us with the awe of Your holiness.
We, too, will praise, glorify, and exalt Your name.

Ruth Brin (adapted)

Untie

Dear God,
We are bound with very tight knots.
They choke off air and stop the blood from pulsating freely.
The knots make us like computers with carefully controlled circuitry.
The knots in our brains tie our creativity—our link with You.
We follow the knot around in its intricacy—but it remains a knot.
The knots in our hearts keep us from crying and dancing when we long to—
They tie us to the posts of the fences that separate us from each other.
The knots in our muscles keep our teeth clenched, our jaws locked, our legs crossed, our shoulders stooped, our backs bent, our chests from inhaling and exhaling the full sweetness of life's breath.
O, God, untie all our knots!

Sheila Peltz Weinberg

Te Deum

Not because of victories
I sing,
having none,
but for the common sunshine,
the breeze,
the largess of the spring,

Not for victory
but for the day's work done
as well as I was able;
not for a seat upon the dais
but at the common table.

Charles Reznikoff

PRELUDES TO KADDISH

To My Father

You gathered incredible strength
in order to die
to seem calm and fully conscious
without complaint, without trembling
without a cry
so that I would not be afraid

Your wary hand
slowly grew cold in mine
and guided me carefully
beyond into the house of death
so I might come to know it

Thus in the past you used to take my hand
and guide me through the world
and show me life
so I would not fear

I will follow after you
confident as a child
toward the silent country
where you went first
so I would not feel a stranger there

And I will not be afraid.

Blaga Dmitrova

Dirge Without Music

I am not resignéd to the shutting away of loving hearts in
the hard ground.
So it is, and so it will be, for so it has been, time out of
mind:
Into the darkness they go, the wise and the lovely. Crowned
With lilies and with laurel they go; but I am not resigned.

Lovers and thinkers, into the earth with you.
Be one with the dull, the indiscriminate dust.
A fragment of what you felt, of what you knew,
A formula, a phrase remains, but the best is lost.

The answers quick and keen, the honest look, the laughter,
the love,
They are gone. They are gone to feed the roses. Elegant and
curled
Is the blossom. Fragrant is the blossom. I know. But I do not
approve.
More precious was the light in your eyes than all the roses in
the world.

Down, down, down into the darkness of the grave
Gently they go, the beautiful, the tender, the kind;
Quietly they go, the intelligent, the witty, the brave.
I know. But I do not approve. And I am not resigned.

Edna St. Vincent Millay

The Intention

Healing is both an exercise
and an understanding
and yet not of the will
nor of the intention
It is a wisdom
and a deeper knowledge
of the daily swing
of life and death
in all creation
There is defeat
to overcome
and acceptance of living
to be established
and always
there must be hope
Not hope of healing
but the hope which informs
the coming moment
and gives it reason
The hope which is
each man's breath
the certainty of love
and of loving
Death may live
in the living
and healing rise
in the dying
for whom the natural end
is part of the gathering
and of the harvest
to be expected
To know healing
is to know that
all life is one

and there is no beginning
and no end
and the intention is loving

Margaret Torrie

The Five Stages of Grief

The night I lost you
someone pointed me towards
the Five Stages of Grief.
Go that way, they said,
it's easy, like learning to climb
stairs after the amputation.
And so I climbed.
Denial was first.
I sat down at breakfast
carefully setting the table
for two. I passed you the toast—
you sat there. I passed
you the paper—you hid
behind it.
Anger seemed more familiar.
I burned the toast, snatched
the paper and read the headlines myself.
But they mentioned your departure
and so I moved on to
Bargaining. What could I exchange
for you? The silence
after storms? My typing fingers?
Before I could decide, Depression
came puffing up, a poor relation
its suitcase tied together
with string. In the suitcase
were bandages for the eyes
and bottles of sleep. I slid

all the way down the stairs
feeling nothing.
And all the time Hope
flashed on and off
in defective neon.
Hope was a signpost pointing
straight in the air.
Hope was my uncle's middle name,
he died of it.
After a year I am still climbing,
though my feet slip
on your stone face.
The treeline
has long since disappeared;
green is a color
I have forgotten.
But now I see what I am climbing
towards: Acceptance
written in capital letters,
a special headline:
Acceptance.
Its name is in lights.
I struggle on,
waving and shouting.
Below, my whole life spreads its surf,
all the landscapes I've ever known
or dreamed of. Below
a fish jumps: the pulse
in your neck
Acceptance. I finally
reach it.
But something is wrong.
Grief is a circular staircase.
I have lost you.

Linda Pastan

ALTERNATIVE PSALM FOR KABBALAT SHABBAT

I Know Not Your Ways

I know not your ways—
A sunset is for me
a godset.
Where are you going,
God?
Take me along,
if, in the "along,"
it is light,
God.

I am afraid of the dark.

Malka Heifetz Tussman (translated from Yiddish)

ZEMIROT / SONGS

Singing together during Shabbat and Festival meals is a beautiful custom. The following is a small selection of traditional and contemporary melodies.

YAH RIBON

זְמִירוֹת

זְמִירוֹת לְשַׁבָּת

יָהּ רִבּוֹן

יָהּ רִבּוֹן עָלַם וְעָלְמַיָּא	Yah ribon alam ve'almaya
אַנְתְּ הוּא מַלְכָּא מֶלֶךְ מַלְכַיָּא:	ant hu malka meleḥ malḥaya.
עוֹבַד גְּבוּרְתֵּךְ וְתִמְהַיָּא	Ovad gevurteḥ vetimhaya
שְׁפַר קֳדָמַי לְהַחֲוָיָה:	shefar kodamay lehaḥavayah.
יָהּ רִבּוֹן עָלַם וְעָלְמַיָּא	Yah ribon alam ve'almaya
אַנְתְּ הוּא מַלְכָּא מֶלֶךְ מַלְכַיָּא:	ant hu malka meleḥ malḥaya.
שְׁבָחִין אֲסַדֵּר צַפְרָא וְרַמְשָׁא:	Shevaḥin asader tzafra veramsha
לָךְ אֱלָהָא קַדִּישָׁא דִּי בְרָא כָּל נַפְשָׁא	laḥ elaha kadisha di vera ḥol nafsha.
עִירִין קַדִּישִׁין וּבְנֵי אֱנָשָׁא	Irin kadishin uvney enasha
חֵיוַת בָּרָא וְעוֹפֵי שְׁמַיָּא:	ḥeyvat bara ve'ofey shemaya.
יָהּ רִבּוֹן עָלַם וְעָלְמַיָּא	Yah ribon alam ve'almaya
אַנְתְּ הוּא מַלְכָּא מֶלֶךְ מַלְכַיָּא:	ant hu malka meleḥ malḥaya.
רַבְרְבִין עוֹבְדָיךְ וְתַקִּיפִין	Ravrevin ovdaḥ vetakifin
מָכֵךְ רָמַיָּא וְזָקֵף כְּפִיפִין	maḥeḥ ramaya vezakef kefifin.
לוּ יְחְיֵא גְבַר שְׁנִין אַלְפִין	Lu yeḥyey gevar shenin alfin
לָא יֵעוֹל גְּבוּרְתֵּךְ בְּחֻשְׁבְּנַיָּא:	la ye'ol gevurteḥ beḥushbenaya.
יָהּ רִבּוֹן עָלַם וְעָלְמַיָּא	Yah ribon alam ve'almaya
אַנְתְּ הוּא מַלְכָּא מֶלֶךְ מַלְכַיָּא: ←	ant hu malka meleḥ malḥaya.

אֱלָהָא דִי לֵהּ יְקָר וּרְבוּתָא	Elaha di ley yekar urvuta
פְּרֹק יָת עָנָךְ מִפֻּם	perok yat anaḥ mipum
אַרְיָוָתָא	aryavata.
וְאַפֵּק יָת עַמָּךְ מִגּוֹ גָלוּתָא	Ve'apek yat amaḥ migo galuta
עַמָּךְ דִי בְחַרְתְּ מִכָּל אֻמַּיָּא:	amaḥ di veḥart mikol umaya.
יָהּ רִבּוֹן עָלַם וְעָלְמַיָּא	Yah ribon alam ve'almaya
אַנְתְּ הוּא מַלְכָּא מֶלֶךְ מַלְכַיָּא:	ant hu malka <u>me</u>leḥ malḥaya.
לְמִקְדְּשָׁךְ תּוּב וּלְקֹדֶשׁ	Lemikdeshaḥ tuv ul<u>ko</u>desh
קֻדְשִׁין	kudshin
אֲתַר דִי בֵהּ יֶחֱדוּן רוּחִין	atar di vey yeḥedun ruḥin
וְנַפְשִׁין	venafshin.
וִיזַמְּרוּן לָךְ שִׁירִין וְרַחֲשִׁין	vizamerun laḥ shirin veraḥashin
בִּירוּשְׁלֵם קַרְתָּא דְשֻׁפְרַיָּא:	birushlem karta deshufraya.
יָהּ רִבּוֹן עָלַם וְעָלְמַיָּא	Yah ribon alam ve'almaya
אַנְתְּ הוּא מַלְכָּא מֶלֶךְ מַלְכַיָּא:	ant hu malka <u>me</u>leḥ malḥaya.

Yah Ribon is a joyous hymn in Aramaic by Israel Najara of Damascus. Written as an acrostic spelling Israel, it recounts the many blessings of God's creation and offers praise to our creator and redeemer. The many and varied tunes to which this song has been put reflect its great popularity among Jews everywhere.

אֶשָּׂא עֵינַי / ESA EYNAY

אֶשָּׂא עֵינַי אֶל־הֶהָרִים	Esa eynay el heharim
מֵאַיִן יָבוֹא עֶזְרִי׃	me'ayin yavo ezri
עֶזְרִי מֵעִם יהוה	ezri me'im adonay
עוֹשֵׂה שָׁמַיִם וָאָרֶץ׃	oseh shamayim va'aretz

I lift my eyes to the hills—
my help comes from there.
My help comes from God,
who makes heaven and earth.

Psalm 121:1–2

YOM ZEH MEḤUBAD

This is a song in honor of Shabbat itself, repeating in poetic form the account of creation and God's rest on Shabbat a day of rejoicing and celebrating the presence of divinity in the world.

יוֹם זֶה מְכֻבָּד

יוֹם זֶה מְכֻבָּד מִכָּל יָמִים כִּי בוֹ שָׁבַת צוּר עוֹלָמִים:

שֵׁשֶׁת יָמִים עֲשֵׂה מְלַאכְתֶּךָ וְיוֹם הַשְּׁבִיעִי לֵאלֹהֶיךָ
שַׁבָּת לֹא תַעֲשֶׂה בוֹ מְלָאכָה כִּי כֹל עָשָׂה שֵׁשֶׁת יָמִים:

יוֹם זֶה מְכֻבָּד מִכָּל יָמִים כִּי בוֹ שָׁבַת צוּר עוֹלָמִים:

רִאשׁוֹן הוּא לְמִקְרָאֵי קֹדֶשׁ יוֹם שַׁבָּתוֹן שַׁבַּת קֹדֶשׁ
עַל כֵּן כָּל אִישׁ בְּיֵינוֹ יְקַדֵּשׁ עַל שְׁתֵּי לֶחֶם יִבְצְעוּ תְמִימִים:

יוֹם זֶה מְכֻבָּד מִכָּל יָמִים כִּי בוֹ שָׁבַת צוּר עוֹלָמִים:

אֱכֹל מַשְׁמַנִּים שְׁתֵה מַמְתַּקִּים כִּי אֵל יִתֵּן לְכֹל בּוֹ דְבֵקִים
בֶּגֶד לִלְבּוֹשׁ לֶחֶם חֻקִּים בָּשָׂר וְדָגִים וְכָל מַטְעַמִּים:

יוֹם זֶה מְכֻבָּד מִכָּל יָמִים כִּי בוֹ שָׁבַת צוּר עוֹלָמִים: ←

Yom zeh meḥubad mikol yamim ki vo shavat tzur olamim.

Sheshet yamim asey melaḥteḥa veyom hashevi'i leyloheḥa
shabbat lo ta'aseh vo melaḥah ki ḥol asah sheshet yamim.

Yom zeh meḥubad mikol yamim ki vo shavat tzur olamim.

Rishon hu limikra'ey kodesh yom shabaton shabbat kodesh
al ken kol ish beyeyno yekadesh al shetey leḥem yivtze'u temimim.

Yom zeh meḥubad mikol yamim ki vo shavat tzur olamim.

Eḥol mashmanim shetey mamtakim ki el yiten leḥol bo devekim
beged lilbosh leḥem ḥukim basar vedagim veḥol matamim.

Yom zeh meḥubad mikol yamim ki vo shavat tzur olamim. ↩

לֹא תֶחְסַר כֹּל בּוֹ וְאָכַלְתָּ וְשָׂבָֽעְתָּ וּבֵרַכְתָּ
אֶת יהוה אֱלֹהֶֽיךָ אֲשֶׁר אָֽהַבְתָּ כִּי בֵרַכְךָ מִכָּל עַמִּים׃

יוֹם זֶה מְכֻבָּד מִכָּל יָמִים כִּי בוֹ שָׁבַת צוּר עוֹלָמִים׃

הַשָּׁמַֽיִם מְסַפְּרִים כְּבוֹדוֹ וְגַם הָאָֽרֶץ מָלְאָה חַסְדּוֹ
רְאוּ כָּל אֵֽלֶּה עָשְׂתָה יָדוֹ כִּי הוּא הַצּוּר פָּעֳלוֹ תָמִים׃

יוֹם זֶה מְכֻבָּד מִכָּל יָמִים כִּי בוֹ שָׁבַת צוּר עוֹלָמִים׃

Lo teḥsar kol bo ve'aḥalta vesavata uveraḥta
et adonay eloheḥa asher ahavta ki veraḥeḥa mikol amim.

Yom zeh meḥubad mikol yamim ki vo shavat tzur olamim.

Hashamayim mesaperim kevodo vegam ha'aretz malah ḥasdo
re'u kol eleh asetah yado ki hu hatzur po'olo tamim.

Yom zeh meḥubad mikol yamim ki vo shavat tzur olamim.

אַחַת שָׁאַ֫לְתִּי / AḤAT SHA'ALTI

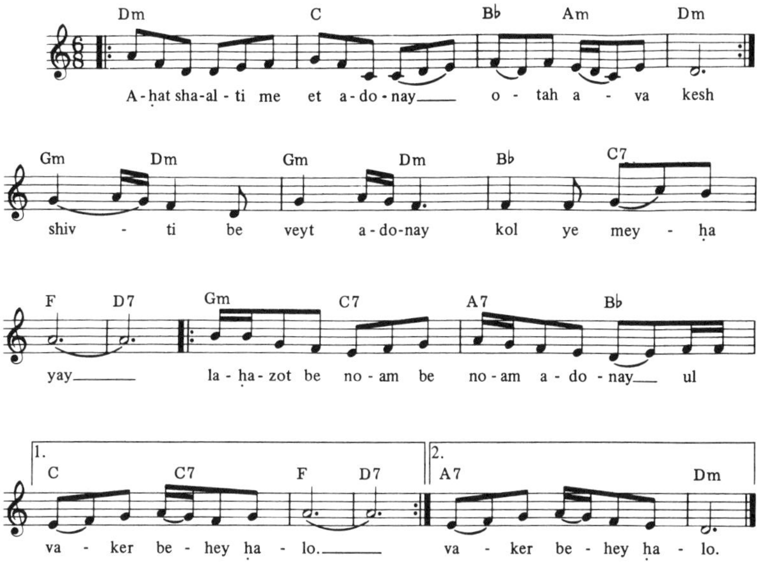

אַחַת שָׁאַ֫לְתִּי מֵאֵת יהוה אוֹתָהּ אֲבַקֵּשׁ
שִׁבְתִּי בְּבֵית יהוה כָּל יְמֵי חַיַּי
לַחֲזוֹת בְּנֹ֫עַם יהוה וּלְבַקֵּר בְּהֵיכָלוֹ:

Aḥat sha'alti me'et adonay otah avakesh
shivti beveyt adonay kol yemey ḥayay
laḥazot beno'am adonay ulvaker beheyḥalo.

One thing I ask from God; one thing do I seek—
that I may stay in the divine presence all the days of my life,
envision divine delight, and contemplate God's presence.

Psalm 27:4

TZUR MISHELO

A song of thanksgiving for the many blessings of God in our lives. The verses of this song follow the order of the paragraphs in *Birkat Hamazon* (the grace after meals), and it serves as an introduction to grace or possibly as an alternative version of it. The song thus includes references to God's feeding and sustaining the world, to the good land that our ancestors were given, to the rebuilding of Zion, and to the coming redemption.

צוּר מִשֶּׁלּוֹ

צוּר מִשֶּׁלּוֹ אָכַלְנוּ בָּרְכוּ אֱמוּנַי שָׂבַעְנוּ וְהוֹתַרְנוּ כִּדְבַר יהוה׃

הַזָּן אֶת עוֹלָמוֹ רוֹעֵנוּ אָבִינוּ אָכַלְנוּ אֶת לַחְמוֹ וְיֵינוֹ שָׁתִינוּ
עַל כֵּן נוֹדֶה לִשְׁמוֹ וּנְהַלְלוֹ בְּפִינוּ אָמַרְנוּ וְעָנִינוּ
אֵין קָדוֹשׁ כַּיהוה׃

צוּר מִשֶּׁלּוֹ אָכַלְנוּ בָּרְכוּ אֱמוּנַי שָׂבַעְנוּ וְהוֹתַרְנוּ כִּדְבַר יהוה׃

בְּשִׁיר וְקוֹל תּוֹדָה נְבָרֵךְ לֵאלֹהֵינוּ עַל אֶרֶץ חֶמְדָּה
שֶׁהִנְחִיל לַאֲבוֹתֵינוּ מָזוֹן וְצֵדָה הִשְׂבִּיעַ לְנַפְשֵׁנוּ
חַסְדּוֹ גָּבַר עָלֵינוּ וֶאֱמֶת יהוה׃

צוּר מִשֶּׁלּוֹ אָכַלְנוּ בָּרְכוּ אֱמוּנַי שָׂבַעְנוּ וְהוֹתַרְנוּ כִּדְבַר יהוה׃ ←

Tzur mishelo aḥalnu bareḥu emunay savanu vehotarnu kidvar adonay.

Ḥazan olamo ro'enu avinu aḥalnu et laḥmo veyeyno shatinu al ken nodeh lishmo unhalelo befinu amarnu ve'aninu eyn kadosh kadonay.

Tzur mishelo aḥalnu bareḥu emunay savanu vehotarnu kidvar adonay.

Beshir vekol todah nevareḥ leloheynu al eretz ḥemdah shehinḥil la'avoteynu mazon vetzedah hisbi'a lenafshenu ḥasdo gavar aleynu ve'emet adonay.

Tzur mishelo aḥalnu bareḥu emunay savanu vehotarnu kidvar adonay. ↵

רַחֵם בְּחַסְדֶּךָ עַל עַמְּךָ צוּרֵנוּ עַל צִיּוֹן מִשְׁכַּן כְּבוֹדֶךָ
זְבוּל בֵּית תִּפְאַרְתֵּנוּ בֶּן דָּוִד עַבְדֶּךָ יָבֹא וְיִגְאָלֵנוּ
רוּחַ אַפֵּינוּ מְשִׁיחַ יהוה:

צוּר מִשֶּׁלּוֹ אָכַלְנוּ בָּרְכוּ אֱמוּנַי שָׂבַעְנוּ וְהוֹתַרְנוּ כִּדְבַר יהוה:

יִבָּנֶה הַמִּקְדָּשׁ עִיר צִיּוֹן תְּמַלֵּא וְשָׁם נָשִׁיר שִׁיר חָדָשׁ
וּבִרְנָנָה נַעֲלֶה הָרַחֲמָן הַנִּקְדָּשׁ יִתְבָּרַךְ וְיִתְעַלֶּה עַל כּוֹס יַיִן מָלֵא
כְּבִרְכַּת יהוה:

צוּר מִשֶּׁלּוֹ אָכַלְנוּ בָּרְכוּ אֱמוּנַי שָׂבַעְנוּ וְהוֹתַרְנוּ כִּדְבַר יהוה:

Raḥem beḥasdeḥa al ameḥa tzurenu al tziyon mishkan kevodeḥa
zevul beyt tifartenu ben david avdeḥa yavo veyigalenu ru'aḥ apeynu meshi'aḥ adonay.

Tzur mishelo aḥalnu bareḥu emunay savanu vehotarnu kidvar adonay.

Yibaneh hamikdash ir tziyon timaley vesham nashir shir ḥadash
uvirnana na'aleh haraḥaman hanikdash yitbaraḥ veyitaleh al kos yayin maley kevirkat adonay.

Tzur mishelo aḥalnu bareḥu emunay savanu vehotarnu kidvar adonay.

יִשְׂמְחוּ הַשָּׁמַיִם / YISMEḤU HASHAMAYIM

יִשְׂמְחוּ הַשָּׁמַיִם	Yismeḥu hashamayim
וְתָגֵל הָאָרֶץ	vetagel ha'aretz
יִרְעַם הַיָּם וּמְלֹאוֹ:	yiram hayam umelo'o.

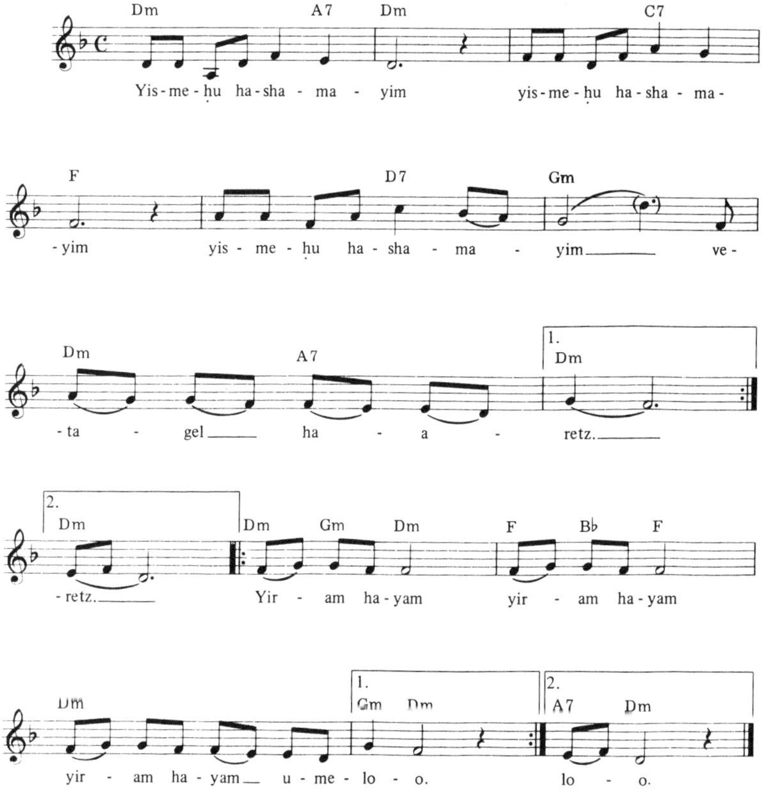

Let the heavens rejoice and the earth be glad,
the sea exult in its fullness.

Psalm 96:11.

MIPI EL

An alphabetical acrostic that sings the praises of God, Moses, the Torah, and Israel. The unusual elevation of Moses in this song is surprising. It may well be a Jewish response to Islamic theology, which insisted on the unique role of its prophet. Such glorification of Moses is well known in medieval Jewish literature.

מִפִּי אֵל

אֵין אַדִּיר כַּיהוה אֵין בָּרוּךְ כְּבֶן עַמְרָם
אֵין גְּדֻלָּה כַּתּוֹרָה אֵין דּוֹרְשֶׁיהָ כְּיִשְׂרָאֵל

מִפִּי אֵל מִפִּי אֵל יְבוֹרָךְ יִשְׂרָאֵל:

אֵין הָדוּר כַּיהוה אֵין וָתִיק כְּבֶן עַמְרָם
אֵין זְכִיָּה כַּתּוֹרָה אֵין חֲכָמֶיהָ כְּיִשְׂרָאֵל

מִפִּי אֵל מִפִּי אֵל יְבוֹרָךְ יִשְׂרָאֵל:

אֵין טָהוֹר כַּיהוה אֵין יָשָׁר כְּבֶן עַמְרָם
אֵין כָּבוֹד כַּתּוֹרָה אֵין לוֹמְדֶיהָ כְּיִשְׂרָאֵל

מִפִּי אֵל מִפִּי אֵל יְבוֹרָךְ יִשְׂרָאֵל: ←

Eyn adir kadonay. Eyn baruḥ keven amram.
Eyn gedulah katorah. Eyn dorsheha keyisra'el.

Mipi el mipi el yevoraḥ yisra'el.

Eyn hadur kadonay. Eyn vatik keven amram.
Eyn zeḥiyah katorah. Eyn ḥaḥameha keyisra'el.

Mipi el mipi el yevoraḥ yisra'el.

Eyn hadur kadonay. Eyn yashar keven amram.
Eyn kavod katorah. Eyn lomdeha keyisra'el.

Mipi el mipi el yevoraḥ yisra'el. ←

אֵין מֶ֫לֶךְ כַּיהוה אֵין נָבִיא כְּבֶן עַמְרָם
אֵין סְגֻלָּה כַּתּוֹרָה אֵין עוֹסְקֶ֫יהָ כְּיִשְׂרָאֵל
מִפִּי אֵל מִפִּי אֵל יְבוֹרַךְ יִשְׂרָאֵל׃

אֵין פּוֹדֶה כַּיהוה אֵין צַדִּיק כְּבֶן עַמְרָם
אֵין קְדֻשָּׁה כַּתּוֹרָה אֵין רוֹמְמֶ֫יהָ כְּיִשְׂרָאֵל
מִפִּי אֵל מִפִּי אֵל יְבוֹרַךְ יִשְׂרָאֵל׃

אֵין קָדוֹשׁ כַּיהוה אֵין רַחוּם כְּבֶן עַמְרָם
אֵין שְׁמִירָה כַּתּוֹרָה אֵין תּוֹמְכֶ֫יהָ כְּיִשְׂרָאֵל
מִפִּי אֵל מִפִּי אֵל יְבוֹרַךְ יִשְׂרָאֵל׃

Eyn meleḥ kadonay. Eyn navi keven amram.
Eyn segulah katorah. Eyn oskeha keyisra'el.
Mipi el mipi el yevoraḥ yisra'el.

Eyn podeh kadonay. Eyn tzadik keven amram.
Eyn kedushah katorah. Eyn romemeha keyisra'el.
Mipi el mipi el yevoraḥ yisra'el.

Eyn kadosh kadonay. Eyn raḥum keven amram.
Eyn shemirah katorah. Eyn tomḥeha keyisra'el.
Mipi el mipi el yevoraḥ yisra'el.

לֹא יִשָּׂא גוֹי / LO YISA GOY

לֹא יִשָּׂא גוֹי אֶל גּוֹי חֶרֶב	Lo yisa goy el goy ḥerev
לֹא יִלְמְדוּ עוֹד מִלְחָמָה׃	Lo yilmedu od milḥamah.

Nation will not lift up sword against nation.
They will not learn war any more.

Isaiah 2:4

YEVAREḤEḤA

Cm Fm G7 Cm
Ye - va-re - ḥe - ḥa ado - nay mi - tzi - yon ur-
Cm7 F/C Fm6/C Cm7 G7 Cm7
-ey be - tuv ye - ru - sha - la - yim ye - va-re - ḥe - ḥa ado-
Fm7 G7 Cm Cm7 Fm6/D G7+5 G7 Cm
-nay mi - tzi - yon kol ye-mey ye-mey ḥa - ye - ḥa
Cm C7 Fm7 B♭7
ur - ey va - nim le - va - ne - ḥa sha - lom al yis - ra-
E♭maj7 G7/D Cm7 C7 Fm
-el ur - ey va - nim le - va - ne - ḥa
1.
Cm B♭7 E♭maj7
sha - lom al yis - ra - el.
2.
Cm/G F/G G7 Cm
sha - lom al yis - ra - el.

יְבָרֶכְךָ

יְבָרֶכְךָ יהוה מִצִּיּוֹן
וּרְאֵה בְּטוּב יְרוּשָׁלָ֫יִם
יְבָרֶכְךָ יהוה מִצִּיּוֹן
כֹּל יְמֵי יְמֵי חַיֶּ֫יךָ׃

וּרְאֵה בָנִים לְבָנֶ֫יךָ
שָׁלוֹם עַל יִשְׂרָאֵל
וּרְאֵה בָנִים לְבָנֶ֫יךָ
שָׁלוֹם עַל יִשְׂרָאֵל׃

Yevareḥeḥa adonay mitziyon
urey betuv yerushalayim
yevareḥeḥa adonay mitziyon
kol yemey yemey ḥayeḥa.

Urey vanim levaneḥa
shalom al yisra'el
urey vanim levaneḥa
shalom al yisra'el.

"May God bless you from Zion
and may you behold the welfare of Jerusalem
all the days of your life.
May you see your children's children;
peace upon Israel."

Psalm 128:5–6

VEHA'ER EYNEYNU

וְהָאֵר עֵינֵינוּ

וְהָאֵר עֵינֵינוּ בְּתוֹרָתֶךָ
וְדַבֵּק לִבֵּנוּ בְּמִצְוֹתֶיךָ
וְיַחֵד לְבָבֵנוּ לְאַהֲבָה
וּלְיִרְאָה אֶת שְׁמֶךָ
שֶׁלֹּא נֵבוֹשׁ וְלֹא נִכָּלֵם
וְלֹא נִכָּשֵׁל לְעוֹלָם וָעֶד:

Veha'er eyneynu betorateḥa
vedabek libenu bemitzvoteḥa
veyaḥed levavenu
le'ahavah ulyirah et shemeḥa
shelo nevosh
velo nikalem
velo nikashel
le'olam va'ed.

Enlighten our eyes with your Torah
and join our hearts with your mitzvot.
Unite our hearts to love
and revere your name.
Thus we will not come to shame or disgrace
and we will not ever stumble.

From *Ahavah Rabah* in the siddur

DODI LI

Refrain:
Dm Gm Dm Gm
Do - di li va - a - ni lo ha - ro - eh
Dm C Dm Dm
ba-sho-sha-nim. Mi zot o - lah min ha - mid-bar
me - ku - te - ret mor mor u - l - vo - nah
Gm C Refrain D.C. Dm C
mi zot o - lah Li - bav - ti - ni a - ḥo - ti ka - lah
mor u - l - vo - nah.
Dm G7 G 1. A 2. A Refrain D.C. Dm
li - bav - ti - ni ka - lah. lah. U - ri
C Dm 1. Dm A7 2. A Refrain D.C.
tza - fon u - vo - i tey - man. man.

דּוֹדִי לִי

דּוֹדִי לִי וַאֲנִי לוֹ	Dodi li va'ani lo
הָרוֹעֶה בַּשּׁוֹשַׁנִּים:	haro'eh bashoshanim.
מִי זֹאת עוֹלָה מִן הַמִּדְבָּר	Mi zot olah min hamidbar
מִי זֹאת עוֹלָה	mi zot olah
מְקֻטֶּרֶת מוֹר וּלְבוֹנָה:	mekuteret mor ulvonah.
דּוֹדִי לִי וַאֲנִי לוֹ	Dodi li va'ani lo
הָרוֹעֶה בַּשּׁוֹשַׁנִּים:	haro'eh bashoshanim.
לִבַּבְתִּינִי אֲחוֹתִי כַלָּה	Libavtini aḥoti kalah
לִבַּבְתִּינִי כַּלָּה:	libavtini kalah.
דּוֹדִי לִי וַאֲנִי לוֹ	Dodi li va'ani lo
הָרוֹעֶה בַּשּׁוֹשַׁנִּים:	haro'eh bashoshanim.
עוּרִי צָפוֹן וּבוֹאִי תֵימָן	Uri tzafon uvo'i teyman
וּבוֹאִי תֵימָן:	uvo'i teyman.
דּוֹדִי לִי וַאֲנִי לוֹ	Dodi li va'ani lo
הָרוֹעֶה בַּשּׁוֹשַׁנִּים:	haro'eh bashoshanim.

My love is mine, and I am his,
who browses in the lotus patch.

Who is this coming up out of the wilderness
perfumed with myrrh and frankincense?

You have enlivened me, my sister-bride.

Awake, north wind,
yes, come, south wind!

A group of verses (2:16, 3:6, 4:9; 4:16) from *Shir Hashirim*

KOL HA'OLAM KULO

כָּל הָעוֹלָם כֻּלּוֹ

כָּל הָעוֹלָם כֻּלּוֹ
גֶּשֶׁר צַר מְאֹד
וְהָעִקָּר לֹא לְפַחֵד כְּלָל׃

Kol ha'olam kulo
gesher tzar me'od
veha'ikar lo lefaḥed kelal.

A saying attributed to Rabbi Naḥman of Bratslav: "The entire world is a very narrow bridge. The main thing is to have no fear at all."

SOURCES

Except as indicated below, all English translation through page 149 is the work of Joel Rosenberg (contemporary poet, essayist, professor of Hebrew Literature and Judaic Studies at Tufts University). All calligraphy and other art work is by Betsy Platkin Teutsch. All comments marked "L.W.K." are from *Arvit LeShabbat,* edited and translated by Levi Weiman-Kelman (contemporary American-Israeli rabbi). Citations for previously published commentary, and full attributions for unpublished material by Mordecai M. Kaplan (American rabbi, 1881–1983; founder of Reconstructionist Judaism), are included below. To avoid confusion, sometimes a title or initial phrase is given. Refer to the key on page vi for full names of commentators. Some biographies of authors of original works appear in the commentary accompanying the text. Others are below. Full credits for outside sources and commentary are located in ACKNOWLEDGMENTS, pages x–xiii.

Pages 4–5

"*Lehadlik nerot* . . . / To light candles . . ." by Zelda (Israeli poet, 1914–1984), with apologies to the translator, whose name we cannot locate.

Page 4

"As the great doors . . ." by Marge Piercy (contemporary American poet and novelist), entitled "Some Blessings."

Page 6

"Blessed is the match . . ." translated from "*Ashrey hagafrur* . . ." by Hannah Szenes (Zionist poet, martyred during World War II), with apologies to the translator, whose name we cannot locate.

"Almighty God . . ." translated for this siddur from the *Shas Tkhines,* an anonymous collection of women's prayers in Yiddish.

Pages 6–11

"*Yedid Nefesh* / Soul Beloved" adapted from a translation by Zalman Schachter-Shalomi. Hebrew original by Eleazar Azikri (sixteenth-century kabbalist). Music traditional.

Page 11

Adapted from Mordecai M. Kaplan, *Judaism Without Supernaturalism,* page 119.

Page 12

"Shabbat Hamalkah / The Shabbat Queen" adapted from an adaptation of a translation by A. Irma Cohon, in *Likrat Shabbat,* page 14.

Page 14

"Shalom Aleyḥem" translated by Burt Jacobson. Music by Israel Goldfarb.

Page 15

"Angels . . ." by Rami M. Shapiro (Reconstructionist rabbi).

Page 31

Adapted from Mordecai M. Kaplan, *Notes on Torah.*

Page 34

Mordecai M. Kaplan, *Notes,* 1920s.

Pages 37 and 41

Adapted from Mordecai M. Kaplan, *Notes,* 1920s.

Page 52

Mordecai M. Kaplan, *Journal,* October 9, 1917.

Page 64

Adapted from Mordecai M. Kaplan, *The Meaning of God in Modern Jewish Religion,* page 248.

Page 65

Ibid., page 249.

Page 66

Adapted from *Ten Rungs: Hasidic Sayings,* collected and edited by Martin Buber (German-Israeli religious philosopher, 1878–1965), page 29.

Page 68

Interpretive Version adapted by Joy D. Levitt from the 1945 Reconstructionist *Sabbath Prayer Book,* pages 28–29.

Page 69

Interpretive Version adapted from "Unending Love" by Rami M. Shapiro (Reconstructionist rabbi), published in *Tangents.*

Page 70

Adapted from Mordecai M. Kaplan, *Notes,* 1920s.

Page 75

"In the handwritten scroll . . ." by Hershel Matt (contemporary American rabbi).

Page 79

Mordecai M. Kaplan, *The Meaning of God in Modern Jewish Religion,* page 172.

Page 79

Adapted from Mordecai M. Kaplan, 1970s.

Page 84

Interpretive Version adapted by Joy D. Levitt from the 1945 Reconstructionist *Sabbath Prayer Book,* pages 38–41.

Page 86

Rami M. Shapiro (Reconstructionist rabbi), "Who is Like You," in *Tangents.*

Page 90

Adapted from Mordecai M. Kaplan, *Notes,* 1940s.

Page 91

"When fears multiply . . ." by Hershel Matt (contemporary American rabbi), published as "Hashkevenu," in *Raayonot,* volume 3, Number 2.

Page 96

"Standing here . . ." by Sandy Eisenberg Sasso (Reconstructionist rabbi).

"Dear God . . ." by Sheila Peltz Weinberg (Reconstructionist rabbi).

Mordecai M. Kaplan, *Diary,* 1904.

Page 97

This Shiviti design is by Betsy Platkin Teutsch, a contemporary American artist, who did all the other artwork in this siddur. The Shiviti is a traditional Jewish art form used for meditation. It is based upon the biblical verse: "I have set (שויתי / Shiviti) Yah always before me" (Psalm 16:8).

Page 98

The quotation made by Levi Weiman-Kelman is from Abraham Joshua Heschel (German-American rabbi and theologian, 1907–1972), *God in Search of Man,* page 201.

Page 100

Adapted from Mordecai M. Kaplan, *Notes.*

Page 101

Rami M. Shapiro (Reconstructionist rabbi), "Receive and Transmit II," in *Tangents.*

Page 104

Mordecai M. Kaplan, *The Meaning of God in Modern Jewish Religion,* page 79.

Page 105

Adapted from *ibid.,* page 103.

Abraham Joshua Heschel (German-American rabbi and theologian, 1907–1972), *The Sabbath: Its Meaning for Modern Man,* page 9.

Page 106

Pinḥas of Koretz was an eighteenth-century Hasidic rabbi.

Page 108

Mordecai M. Kaplan, *The Meaning of God in Modern Jewish Religion,* page 360.

Page 109

Abraham Joshua Heschel (German-American rabbi and theologian, 1907–1972), *God in Search of Man,* pages 49 and 48.

Page 114

Adapted from *The Meaning of God in Modern Jewish Religion,* page 165.

Page 116

Adapted from *ibid.,* page 81.

Page 126

"The commandment . . ." by Sandy Eisenberg Sasso (Reconstructionist rabbi).

Page 132

Mordecai M. Kaplan, "Sermon at S.A.J.," 1922.

"As the hand . . ." adapted from *Ten Rungs: Hasidic Sayings,* collected and edited by Martin Buber (German-Israeli religious philosopher, 1878–1965), page 39.

Page 135

"When senseless hatred . . ." adapted from *ibid.,* page 79.

Adapted from Mordecai M. Kaplan, *S.A.J. Review,* 1928.

Page 136

Alternative Version by Rami M. Shapiro (Reconstructionist rabbi), published as "It Is Up To Us " in *Tangents.*

Page 137

Alternative Version by Judy Chicago (contemporary American artist and poet), entitled "Merger." Capitalization is identical to that in the original.

Page 142

Mordecai M. Kaplan, *Journal,* 1933.

Pages 150–178

The passages in the Interpretive Amidah were written or (as listed below) selected by Marcia Falk (contemporary American poet). They will appear in Marcia Falk, *The Book of Blessings,* 1990 (forthcoming, Harper & Row). All translations in this section are by Marcia Falk.

Pages 152–153

Leah Goldberg (Hebrew Poet, 1911–1970), "*Mibeyt Imi* / From My Mother's House."

Pages 154–155

Malka Heifetz Tussman (Yiddish-American poet, 1896–1987), "*A Yingling Mit An Eppel in Hant* / Eating An Apple."

Page 156–158

Malka Heifetz Tussman (Yiddish-American poet, 1896–1987), "*Ikh Bin Froy* / I Am Woman."

Page 161

Leah Goldberg (Hebrew Poet, 1911–1970), "*Beḥol davar yesh lefaḥot sheminit . . .* / In everything, there is at least an eighth . . ."

Page 162–163

Zelda (Israeli poet, 1914–1984), "*Hakarmel Ha'inireh* / The Invisible Carmel."

Page 164

Malka Heifetz Tussman (Yiddish-American poet, 1896–1987), "*Bletter* / Leaves."

Pages 166–167

Zelda (Israeli poet, 1914–1984), "Each of Us Has a Name," translated from "*Leḥol Ish Yesh Shem,*" in *Shirey Zelda.*

Page 169

Zelda (Israeli poet, 1914–1984), "*Hadliku Ner* / Light a Candle."

Page 177

Zelda (Israeli poet, 1914–1984), "*Hageshem Harishon . . .* / The first rain . . ."

Pages 179–183

Amidah Meditations composed by Devora Bartnoff (Reconstructionist rabbi).

Page 184

A Short Amidah, by Syd Lieberman (contemporary American storyteller and poet), published as "The Amidah" in *Raayonot,* volume 3, Number 2.

Pages 186–187

Kadia Molodowsky (Yiddish poet, 1894–1975), "Song of the Sabbath," translated by Jean Valentine, in *A Treasury of Yiddish Poetry.*

Pages 187–188

Marge Piercy (contemporary American poet and novelist), "Wellfleet Sabbath," in *Available Light.*

Pages 188–189

Abraham Joshua Heschel (German-American rabbi and theologian, 1907–1972), *The Insecurity of Freedom.*

Pages 189–190

Adapted from Mordecai M. Kaplan, *The Meaning of God in Modern Jewish Religion,* pages 57–58.

Pages 190–191

Shmuel Hanagid (medieval Spanish poet and statesman), translated in the *Society Hill Synagogue Prayer Supplement,* edited by Ivan Caine.

Pages 191–192

Adapted by Lee Friedlander from "Where We Can Find God," in the 1945 Reconstructionist *Sabbath Prayer Book,* pages 343–347. This poem is translated by Eugene Kohn from a Hebrew adaptation by David Frischmann of Tagore's "Gitanjali." Rabindranath Tagore was a modern Indian poet and mystic.

Pages 192–194

Adapted by Lee Friedlander from Mordecai M. Kaplan, "God The Life of Nature," in the 1945 Reconstructionist *Sabbath Prayer Book,* pages 383–391.

Pages 194–195

Ruth Brin (contemporary American poet), "In Praise / GENESIS 1,2" in *Harvest: Collected Poems and Prayers.*

Pages 195–196

Howard Nemerov (contemporary American poet), "Trees," in *The Collected Poems of Howard Nemerov.*

Page 196

Wendell Berry (contemporary American poet), "The Peace of Wild Things," in *Collected Poems.*

Pages 196–197

Adapted from Mordecai M. Kaplan, *The Meaning of God in Modern Jewish Religion,* page 266.

Pages 197–199

Ruth H. Sohn (contemporary American rabbi), "I Shall Sing to the Lord a New Song."

Pages 199–200

Merle Feld (contemporary American poet and playwright), "We All Stood Together."

Page 200

Michael Walzer (contemporary American political philosopher), *Exodus and Revolution,* page 149.

Pages 200–201

Adapted from Mordecai M. Kaplan, *Notes.*

Pages 201–202

Nelly Sachs (German poet, 1891–1970), "We Mothers," translated by Ruth and Matthew Mead, in *The Seeker.*

Page 202

Yehuda Amichai (contemporary Israeli poet), "An Appendix To The Vision of Peace," translated by Glenda Abramson and Tudor Parfitt, in *Great Tranquility: Questions and Answers.*

Pages 202–203

Yehuda Amichai (contemporary Israeli poet), "Wildpeace," translated by Chana Bloch and Ariel Bloch, in *Tikkun,* volume 2, number 2.

Page 203

Adapted from Albert Einstein.

Page 204

Adapted from Ruth Brin (contemporary American poet), "A Sense of Your Presence," in *Harvest.*

Page 205

Sheila Peltz Weinberg (Reconstructionist rabbi), "Untie."

Page 205

Charles Reznikoff (American poet, 1894–1976), "Te Deum," in *Poems 1937–1975,* volume ii.

Page 206

Blaga Dmitrova, "To My Father."

Page 207

Edna St. Vincent Millay (modern American poet), "Dirge Without Music," in *Collected Poems.*

Pages 208–209

Margaret Torrie (contemporary American poet), "The Intention," in *All in the End is Harvest.*

Pages 209–210

Linda Pastan (contemporary American poet), "The Five Stages of Grief," in *The Five Stages of Grief.*

Page 211

Malka Heifetz Tussman (Yiddish-American poet, 1896–1987), "I Know Not Your Ways," translated by Marcia Falk.

Pages 212–235

Commentary on *zemirot* is by Arthur Green (President of the Reconstructionist Rabbinical College).

Pages 212–214

"*Yah Ribon.*" Words by Israel Najara of Damascus (Hebrew poet of the sixteenth century). Hasidic melody.

Page 215

"*Esa Eynay.*" Music by Shlomo Carlebach.

Pages 216–218

"*Yom Zeh Meḥubad.*" Hasidic melody.

Page 219

"*Aḥat Sha'alti.*" Folk tune.

Pages 220–222

"*Tzur Mishelo.*" Ladino folk tune.

Page 223

"*Yismeḥu Hashamayim.*" Hasidic melody.

Pages 224–226

"*Mipi El.*" Oriental folk tune.

Page 227

"*Lo Yisa Goy.*" Music by Shalom Altman.

Pages 228–229

"*Yevareḥeḥa.*" Music by David Weinkrantz.

Pages 230–231

"*Veha'er Eyneynu.*" Music by Shlomo Carlebach.

Pages 232–233

"*Dodi Li.*" Music by Nira Chen.

Pages 234–235

"*Kol Ha'olam Kulo.*" Lyrics by Naḥman of Bratslav (eighteenth-century Hasidic rebbe). Music by Baruch Chait.

PUBLISHER'S NOTE

This book is published by the Reconstructionist Press, which is sponsored by the Federation of Reconstructionist Congregations and Havurot. The FRCH also publishes the *Reconstructionist* magazine. Founded in 1954, the FRCH is the lay arm of the Reconstructionist movement. The FRCH does outreach, provides a variety of services to its congregations, and does regional and movement-wide programming.

To order copies of this book, or to obtain book lists or other information, please contact:

Federation of Reconstructionist Congregations
and Havurot
Church Road and Greenwood Avenue
Wyncote, PA 19095–1898

(215) 887–1988